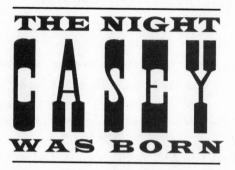

Also by John Evangelist Walsh

*Walking Shadows: Orson Welles,
William Randolph Hearst, and Citizen Kane.*

The Execution of Major Andre

Moonlight: Abraham Lincoln and the Almanac Trial

Darkling I Listen: The Last Days and Death of John Keats

Midnight Dreary: The Mysterious Death of Edgar Allan Poe

*Unraveling Piltdown: The Science Fraud
of the Century and its Solution*

*The Shadows Rise: Abraham Lincoln and the
Anne Rutledge Legend*

This Brief Tragedy: Unraveling the Todd-Dickinson Affair

Into My Own: The English Years of Robert Frost

*The Bones of St. Peter: A Full Account of the Search
for the Apostle's Body*

*Plumes In the Dust: The Love Affair of
Edgar Allan Poe and Fanny Osgood*

Night on Fire: John Paul Jones' Greatest Battle

*One Day at Kitty Hawk: The Untold Story of the
Wright Brothers and the Airplane*

The Hidden Life of Emily Dickinson

*Poe the Detective: The Curious Circumstances
Behind The Mystery of Marie Roget*

*Strange Harp, Strange Symphony:
The Life of Francis Thompson*

The Letters of Francis Thompson (Collected, Annotated)

The Shroud: The Story of the Holy Shroud of Turin

Fiction

The Man Who Buried Jesus: A Mystery Novel

Frontis: The Polo Grounds, New York Giants Opening Day, April 25, 1888. Giants in white uniforms at the left, Philadelphia Phillies in black at the right. Somewhere along the first base line sits DeWolf Hopper, the actor (The standing figure in light gray, section 2 from left, may be him. See page 34 for an enlargement.). Four months later at Wallack's Theater he will give the first public recital of Casey at the Bat, *launching the ballad on its fabulous career.*

THE NIGHT
CASEY
WAS BORN

JOHN EVANGELIST WALSH

THE TRUE STORY BEHIND THE
GREAT AMERICAN BALLAD

"CASEY AT THE BAT"

THE OVERLOOK PRESS

WOODSTOCK & NEW YORK

This edition first published in the United States in 2007 by
The Overlook Press, Peter Mayer Publishers, Inc.
Woodstock & New York

WOODSTOCK:
One Overlook Drive
Woodstock, NY 12498
www.overlookpress.com
[for individual orders, bulk and special sales, contact our Woodstock office]

NEW YORK:
141 Wooster Street
New York, NY 10012

Cataloging-in-Publication Data is available from the Library of Congress

Book design and type formatting by Bernard Schleifer
Manufactured in the United States of America
ISBN-13 978-1-58567-893-8
10 9 8 7 6 5 4 3 2 1

PROGRAM

ILLUSTRATIONS

For my grandson,
ANDREW WALSH,
who might have made a
great first baseman,
but who prefers,
and is a whiz at,
soccer

OVERTURE
ON STAGE AND FIELD

AFTER HE'D SPENT ALMOST HALF A CENTURY PERFORMING and was nearing his seventieth birthday, the great old-time comic opera star DeWolf Hopper indulged himself in a wry confession. "When my name is called upon the resurrection morn," he sighed, "I shall probably, unless some friend is there to pull the sleeve of my ascension robe, clear my throat and begin, 'The outlook wasn't brilliant for the Mudville nine that day.'"

From his hearers, all aware that it was only a slight exaggeration, the remark brought knowing nods and appreciative smiles. Hopper wasn't in the least complaining, they knew. During some forty years, beginning one memorable night in 1888, he had, by his own casual estimate, charmed audiences with the grand old baseball ballad, *Casey at the Bat*, no fewer than ten thousand times, a figure often quoted. (Much too high, of course, calling for a performance five times a week every week, unfailingly, for four decades. More like it would be less than half that total, still remarkable.) In theaters all over the country, as a feature added to the night's regular bill or as a curtain call, and on many hundreds of other occasions, formal and informal, he'd delighted audiences with his captivating rendition of the poem's fifty-two sprightly lines about the dismal failure of Mudville's mighty slugger.

He didn't docilely "recite" the poem. He dramatized it vocally, almost "performed" it. For him the poem was not a mere literary text, it was an actual script for a one-act comedy with action and dialogue all neatly laid out, and involving several characters besides Casey and the umpire. Solely by giving free rein to his wonderfully flexible baritone voice, his large, mobile features mirroring the words, he created a stadium filled with excited fans, his broadly varied delivery bringing to vivid life the very personality of the celebrated slugger.

In the 118 years since Hopper's first on-stage performance of the poem it has garnered an amazing amount of attention. Separately and in collections it has been endlessly reprinted, probably more than any other single piece of fugitive verse (its only competition would be C.C. Moore's *The Night Before Christmas*, and perhaps Poe's *The Raven*). It has been imitated, parodied, plagiarized, fictionalized, dramatized in song and story, set to music as a popular song, and often recited on radio. It has been made into three movies (silent), one starring Hopper himself, and one Wallace Beery. It has been recorded by some dozen performers, again including Hopper (three times, all of which this writer has studied with delight). It has been painted, sketched, and sculpted by an army of professional artists, and made into picture books for juveniles—one recent version for children won the prestigious Caldecott Award. In 1953 it reached a level that its most devoted admirers couldn't have predicted: It was made into a serious, if small-scale opera, with a chorus of fifty (music by William Schumann, libretto by Jerome Gury). It has also been the basis for a full-scale ballet.

Hopper was not the poem's author, but without him the familiar mock-heroic portrait of the great Casey—like a monarch "advancing to the bat," in his lordly way calming "the maddened thousands" in the stands after he'd taken two strikes, then ingloriously striking out—might never have become the classic that it is: baseball's favorite poem and America's best-known, best-loved comic ballad.

Not to be slighted is the poem's own peculiar literary excellence, a factor not always admitted or remembered. At first blush it may seem to lack that quality of "high seriousness" supposed to underlie superior poetry, but it's there, all right, a goodly portion of it, between and behind the lines, quietly assumed, for otherwise the poem wouldn't work at all. High seriousness! If the true baseball fan feels serious about anything it's that moment of nerve-wracking anticipation when, as in the poem, his team is behind in late innings, the bases are loaded, and the Great Man is coming up! Judged on its own level, in tone, pace, nuance, descriptive power, sharpness of imagery, and prosodic skill, *Casey* is every bit the equal of loftier works, a Kipling ballad, say, or a Browning soliloquy. Ranging it beside Whittier's *Barefoot Boy*, or parts of his *Snowbound*, or something of Frost's, his *Mending Wall* or *Birches*, is no great exaggeration. Some of Wordsworth's things are not out of reach.

Despite Hopper, a lesser composition would never have gained for its hero the stature in America's consciousness—

along with such as Paul Bunyan, John Henry, and Johnny Appleseed—achieved by *Casey*.

Remarkably, the poem's author, Ernest L. Thayer—a Massachusetts man and only twenty-four years old when he wrote the poem—produced nothing else that comes near his masterpiece. His other poems, or *ballads*, as he liked to call them—all newspaper contributions—are little more than glib attempts to appear wittily knowing on a variety of topics. Thayer is a prime example of that strange breed, the one-poem poet, no surprise, really, for in *Casey*, he treated a subject he knew well, and did so at a time when he was in some turmoil of spirit over his uncertain future, including a recently failed love affair. *Casey* it seems, was the frustrated Thayer's momentary escape from personal confusion and doubt back into a pleasanter, more settled and familiar world. Personal in nature, very much of its own time, it still exudes a permanent, universal appeal.

Hopper himself was an avid baseball fan—in 1888 they were called "cranks"—a staunch New York Giants rooter. "The biggest baseball crank in the country," the Chicago *Tribune* styled him. Whenever he was playing the New York theaters and the Giants were at home he attended the games, all played at the old Polo Grounds at the northern tip of Central Park (110th Street and Fifth Avenue), an hour's carriage ride uptown from the Broadway theaters. With friend and fellow-actor Digby Bell, he was, as he said, "at the Polo Grounds every free afternoon."

Without his association with the poem, it is sometimes claimed, Hopper might have been little known and soon forgotten. The truth is that for an entire generation, beginning

DeWolf Hopper and fellow actor Digby Bell often rode the Broadway Stage from the downtown theaters, where they were playing, up to the old Polo Grounds at 110th Street and Fifth Avenue to attend New York Giants games.

in 1885 when he joined the McCaull Light Opera Company in New York, Hopper was a headliner, known for his vocal artistry and his genius both as an actor and a funny man. It was in his later years as his star waned that *Casey* was of most value to him, serving as a virtuoso piece to be given anywhere at any time, like a Shakespearean actor who could on demand trot out *To Be or Not to Be* (which, come to think of it, can be read as a neat little comment on *Casey*!).

The fabled stage beauty Lillian Russell, a Hopper co-star in the Nineties, recalled the off-stage man she knew and greatly admired: "He is as perennial as the spring, as delightful too and as refreshing. He is one of the most deeply educated men of our profession. He not only is a thinker but he is a scholar and student as well, with his knowledge divided between books and human nature. . . . As a public speaker he has no equal. I never heard such a flow of language as he can send forth without the slightest effort. He can hold a thousand with the spell of his voice as easily as he can hold one."

The very first of Hopper's numerous performances of the poem took place soon after its initial appearance in print, in June 1888 in an obscure California newspaper. The occasion was a special "Baseball Night" that August at Wallack's Theater in New York, where he was appearing in a Johann Strauss operetta, *Prince Methusalem*. At the time a hot, three-way pennant race was in progress in the National League, involving the New York Giants under their great catcher Buck Ewing, the Chicago White Stockings led by the formidable Cap Anson, and Boston, led by the one-and-only Mike "King" Kelly. It was the excitement of the pennant race that inspired Wallack's baseball night, at which the New York and Chicago teams were present as honored guests, indirectly setting the stage for *Casey*, a last-minute addition to the bill. How the poem so quickly found its way from far-off Frisco to Broadway, and into the hands of the one man able to do it justice as a recital piece, is not the least beguiling part of the great ballad's history.

Surprising, in view of the massive, long-time attention given the poem, is the fact that the full story of that famous first night at Wallack's Theater when the twenty-nine-year-old Hopper first recited it in public, has never been told. Nor has the story of what led up to the occasion, and what followed, been at all well covered. But surely the premier of the immortal *Casey* is as eminently worthy of notice, of preservation, as any of history's major debuts, for instance the gala opening of the Brooklyn Bridge, with fireworks that lit up New York, or the dramatic unsealing of King Tut's tomb, or the activation of the Atlantic cable. That this present book is the first one to gather together the whole story in detail of the poem's authorship, its landmark entry as a showpiece at Wallack's, its fortunes since then, and the facts about the two gifted men behind it all—well, we can only shake our heads at history's incomprehensible lapses.

The different chapters I call "scenes" in recognition of the fact that the theater played as large a role in *Casey*'s fortunes as did any ball park, or printing press. But in these scenes will be found not the least taint of fiction, only witnessed historical truth. The documents behind the story, the authentic sources for all that is pictured or suggested in these scenes, we'll herd together at the book's rear: safe and conveniently out of the way, they may be ignored by any reader so inclined.

As to my title, *The Night Casey Was Born*. The fact, of course, is that *Casey* had a double entrance into this world, enjoyed the luxury of two births, one when the poem was written, and again when Hopper brought it to vivid life before an audience. In these pages I tell the story of both births in a single narrative which recaptures—so I hope—something of the original glow that lit long-ago reality.

THE NIGHT CASEY WAS BORN

"Mr. Speaker. . . . On this auspicious occasion the lyric strains of *Casey at the Bat* should be included in the record of this day's proceedings so that my colleagues may reflect on its profound sentiments."

—REP. TOM LANTOS *addressing the House of Representatives on the 100th anniversary of the poem's publication.*

1

THE POLO GROUNDS, NEW YORK, OPENING DAY, APRIL 1888

I
N THE SURGING, CHATTERING CROWD OF DERBY-HATTED, dark-suited men streaming through the high, arched portal of the ball park, the light, stylish bowler of one unusually tall, gray-suited figure rose high above the rest. Beside him, talking excitedly, hurried a smaller man, the top of whose derby barely reached to his companion's shoulder.

Once inside the gate the two did not head for their seats in the double-decked wooden pavilion. Instead, they turned and entered a side doorway, then went along a narrow corridor, and halted at another door, this one blocked by a guard. "Afternoon, Mr. Hopper. Afternoon Mr. Bell," said the guard politely as he reached behind him to push open the door of the Giants' dressing room.

It was April 25, 1888, the home opener for New York's National League team. The very tall DeWolf Hopper and his shorter companion Digby Bell, both leading members of the McCaull Light Opera Company, were fervent followers of baseball. Determined not to miss the season opener, they had wangled a few hours away from the rehearsals for their new show then going on down at Wallack's Theater on lower Broadway. They had detoured to the Giants' dressing room to say a quick word of encouragement to their good friends, manager Jim Mutrie and team captain Buck Ewing, and to wish each of the players good luck.

Inside, they found the room loudly abuzz with talk as some twenty men changed from street clothes into playing togs (white uniforms with dark stockings, dark belts, and dark collars, high-topped leather shoes, and flat, squared-off caps, also white). Recognized by the players, the two were warmly greeted as they went round the room renewing acquaintances interrupted since the previous October, shaking hands and cracking jokes about the Philadelphia players, the Giants' opening day opponents.

Now in the league for six years—the league itself went back only to 1876—the Giants had yet to come out on top. In their first five years they'd finished sixth, fourth, second, third, and again fourth. This year, Hopper loudly predicted, would be the year! Bell happily agreed.

First along the line of wooden lockers was the very tough and versatile Ewing, the regular catcher, but who alternated at third. Today he'd be playing third. Catching would be the veteran, Orator O'Rourke, at thirty-eight still among the league's best hitters and excellent on defense (his real name was Jim but he had a forceful voice and manner and did all the team's serious talking). Next came right-fielder Mike Tiernan—"Silent Mike"—the youngest player at twenty-one. A great fielder and a feared hitter, he almost never had anything to say but hello, goodbye, yes, no, and maybe. Then came Monte Ward, a top man at shortstop and at bat.

DeWolf Hopper (right) and his baseball pal, fellow-actor Digby Bell. The two were prominent members of the McCaull Light Opera Company, based in New York City. Together they often attended games at the old Polo Grounds.

Brainiest and best-educated of all the players, he had a law degree and practiced in the off-season.

Next was Danny Richardson who sparkled at second base, and left-fielder Mike Slattery, and center fielder Elmer Foster (a utility man today taking the place of the ailing Tom Brown). The starting pitcher turned out to be, not the marvelous Tim Keefe, as expected, but Mickey Welch, only a little behind Keefe as a strike-out artist. Both men were given hearty handshakes by the actors.

Last was first baseman Roger Conner, big and brawny but a man of smiling, easy-going disposition. Tall for the time at 6'3", rising to take Hopper's outstretched hand he had to look up a little to meet the eyes of the actor, who stood a couple of inches taller.

One of the league's two premier power hitters (Dan Brouthers of Detroit was the other), Connor also hit for average, and had already won one batting title (.371). In the previous season he'd blasted seventeen home runs, only two behind the league leader. People were still talking about the one he'd hit clear out of the Polo Grounds, the first and only time it had ever been done. Sailing over the far center-field fence, it traveled more than 400 feet. (With today's livelier ball it would certainly have gone over 600 feet. Later that year in an exhibition game he blasted one a measured 460 feet.) Very fast for a big man, in the past five years he'd also hit an amazing seventy-six triples. (Today he is still No. 5, all-time, in triples, with 233.) As a home-run hitter he would become the career leader with 138, a mark that would fall only to Babe Ruth. His flashiest feat so far was to pole three long-distance home-runs in one game.

(The so-called "dead ball" of the time did not make for a less exciting game, but often more exciting, and the home-run played its regular, if less frequent part. With the dead ball—less resilient—there was more movement on the field, more continuous action, and more complications in the play—"the inside game," they called it. But a fan of today watching a game in progress back then would not be able to spot much real difference in the physical action. Running, hitting, throwing, pitching, tactics, strategy, aggressive, coordinated play, three strikes and out—though five balls for a walk, not four—were all pretty much the same in 1888 as now.)

At the room's center stood manager Mutrie with a shiny black topper perched a little back on his head. Like many accomplished men of the time he customarily wore a top-hat, and almost never removed it, not even on the field or in the dug-out during a game. Hopper and Bell, finishing their rounds, were just talking with him when there came wafting into the dressing room the sounds of martial music. The U.S. Army's Seventh Regiment Band had struck up, signaling the start of the opening ceremonies. Bidding everyone a final good luck, the two actors hurried out to find their box seats along the first-base line.

Two hours later the game was over and the once-noisy crowd of Giants rooters began quietly to disperse. From the field the white-suited New York players drifted dejectedly back to the dressing room, while the black-suited Philadelphians laughed, hollered, and congratulated each other. They'd won handily, beating the over confident Giants 5-3.

*Jim Mutrie (above) in 1888 was serving his fourth year as Giants
manager. Buck Ewing (facing page), great all-rounder, was in his
sixth year as Giants catcher. Both were good friends of DeWolf
Hopper.*

There'd been no heavy hitting in the game, but several moments of real excitement. In the eighth the Giants, trailing by 2-1, tied the score when Connor walked, stole second, and came in on Ward's double. The Phillies snapped right back when an error by Ward allowed two men to cross the plate. In fact there were a surprising number of errors on both sides: for Philly a total of nine, for the Giants no fewer than eleven.

That spotlights a main difference between the baseball of the 1880s and what came later: the players didn't use gloves, but caught and fielded the ball barehanded. As a result, split, sprained and broken fingers were not uncommon. Routine were bruised flesh, sore tendons, and aching palms.

A few players had begun to use gloves, small, makeshift, and clumsily padded. They were laughed at as sissies, and most players still felt that the bare hand gave more control of the speeding ball. Even catchers had yet to adopt padded gloves, wearing only ordinary thick, unpadded leather gloves with the fingers cut out. More than twenty games without a break was unusual for a catcher.

Playing barehanded inevitably led to errors—dropped flys, booted grounders, and fumbled catches, with aching hands causing wayward throws. So taken for granted at the time were errors as a normal part of play that box scores prominently featured a column marked "E," toting up a team's miscues, player by player with the figure at the bottom almost never showing as a zero. The twenty errors committed in the 1888 Polo Grounds opener were not thought excessive. After all, it was the season's first game, and hands grown soft over the winter had to be toughened up.

Hopper and Bell, while sorely disappointed at the loss, could not linger at the field to rehash the game or commiserate with the chagrined Mutrie. Having indulged themselves by remaining until the last out, they were now in a hurry to get back to the theater, and from the Polo Grounds, Wallack's lay an hour's carriage ride away by the regular Fifth Avenue stage. A ponderous, four-horse vehicle holding some twenty passengers comfortably, it provided a slow, meandering if pleasant ride down through the sylvan vistas of Central Park. At 59th Street, though, the park ended and the noisy clutter of lower New York began, with its jumbled, clogging horse-drawn traffic further slowing progress. Opening night for the new operetta was only ten days off. Colonel McCaull would not be amused if he had to wait too long for the return of his two stars.

The new operetta, titled *The Lady or the Tiger?*, had been written by an American team, the veteran librettist Sydney Rosenfeldt, and the respected composers Julius Lyons and Adolph Nowak. The huge popularity of operetta (comic opera, people called it, or light opera) in the country then was a fairly recent development, actually a bare dozen years old (like professional baseball itself!). The boom had begun with the importation of foreign works—Viennese, German, French, and English (mostly Gilbert and Sullivan). American composers and writers had begun to catch up with the foreign competition but still had not gained the favor accorded works by the Europeans. *The Lady or the Tiger?* it was hoped would score a real triumph for the

American musical theater, opening the way for the native product. Not least among its qualifications was the cast, built around Hopper, Jefferson De Angelis, Mathilda Cottrelly, and Eugene Oudin. None of the four could be said to have reached full-fledged stardom as yet, able to carry a show on the strength of a name. But taken together McCaull's was acknowledged to be the finest troupe of actors and singers on Broadway. Of the four, Hopper's name stood highest, on the edge of real stardom.

The new show's plot, unlike most operettas, would itself be a drawing card, or so all expected. It was based on a short story, barely six pages in length, by a leading American author, Frank R. Stockton, and had originally appeared in 1882 in *Century* magazine. The tantalizing tale was much discussed, becoming a topic of jest and earnest argument at New York's cafes and dinner tables. In the story, an ancient king devises a situation which results in his own daughter becoming involved in the fate of her illicit lover, who has been rejected and condemned by the king. The lover is taken to an arena where he must choose between two doors. Behind one is a ferocious tiger ready to pounce. Behind the other is a beautiful maiden whom the lover, if he chooses that door, must immediately marry. From that condition there is no appeal: the wedding must take place on the spot.

The King's daughter manages to discover which door is which, and at the last moment from the stands she secretly signals her lover to choose the door on the right. This the trusting lover proceeds to do: "And so I leave it to all of you," abruptly concludes the original tale. "Which came out of the opened door—the lady, or the tiger?"

If the printed story deliberately and tantalizingly left the question unanswered, the operetta, offering two hours' worth of song, dance, and comedy, boldly supplied it. Revelation of who or what came out of the opened door would provide the show's climactic moment. Colonel McCaull made sure that the fact, but not the solution, was well advertised to the paying public.

By now for the busily rehearsing Hopper, baseball was out. No more trips up to the Polo Grounds, not for a while. Three more games were played in the series between the Giants and Philadelphia (New York took all three). Then Boston, New York's bitterest rival, came in for a round of four games. After Boston, New York City would have no baseball for several weeks, the Giants leaving on their initial "western" trip (at that time no further than Detroit, Indianapolis, Chicago).

The Boston games, especially, with the celebrated Mike "King" Kelly performing, Hopper and his friends yearned to see. Whenever King Kelly came to town attendance at the games jumped a couple of thousand. But with opening night looming so close they had little hope of getting away from rehearsals. All day and every day now, and most evenings, they were expected to be at the theater for a last run-through of songs, scenes, costume fittings, and endless make-up sessions, all pointing toward a final, full-dress rehearsal on May 6, the day before the premier.

Unable to go up to the games they did the next best thing, closely following the Giants' fortunes, and Kelly's

This photograph of the Polo Grounds on Opening Day, 1888, is an enlargement of a section in the frontispiece. It probably shows DeWolf Hopper and Digby Bell in the stands at center background. Five figures in the stands at that location are obviously posed: the standing, gray-suited figure (Hopper), the dark-hatted man behind him (Bell), and the three men seated on the railing in front of them (unidentified). Hopper and Bell were good friends of Giants manager Mutrie and the players, and were often at Giants games at the Polo Grounds. Including them in the Opening Day photo would have been quite natural.

exploits, in two or three newspapers. What they read would have made them even sorrier that they weren't there to see it. The unstoppable Kelly really did put on a show.

Each team won two of the four games played. For the Boston victories Kelly was the whole difference, and he came near pulling out a third win. In the first Boston victory he began the scoring on a wild dash home from third that ended in one of his famous hook slides, a style he perfected if he didn't invent it. He also scored the runs that tied, then won the game. Boston lost the second game and Kelly managed only two walks and a stolen base. The third game was also a Boston loss, in which Kelly lashed a two-run homer to left for his team's only runs. Boston won the fourth game with Kelly scoring twice, and his work behind the plate—he alternated between right field and catcher—the *Times* called "a feature of the game."

If Hopper and Bell on the cluttered rehearsal stage of Wallack's Theater were pausing between practice turns to read of the King's heroics at the Polo Grounds, another young man, in Worcester, Massachusetts—some 150 miles due north of New York City—was reading about the same games but in a paper closer to home, the Boston *Globe.* (It gave Kelly a good deal more space than did the New York papers.) A long-time resident of Worcester, he was a quiet, well-spoken twenty-four-year-old, a budding journalist given to writing poetry, what he preferred to call "ballads." In the first days of May 1888, with the baseball season barely a month old, he'd just begun writing another one. It told of an exciting game played in a town he named Mudville.

2
A LARGE RESIDENCE, WORCESTER, MASSACHUSETTS, MAY 1888

ITTING AT THE DESK IN HIS STUDY, TOYING ABSENTLY WITH a pencil, the young man gazed dreamily out the window at the gray landscape just beginning to kindle in the Massachusetts spring. The house, a large and elegant structure bespeaking wealth, stood at No. 67 Chatham Street in Worcester, forty miles due west of Boston.

His was the classic dilemma, thought the young man ruefully. A problem not rare and never easily solved among the sons of privilege.

In the three years that had passed since his graduation from Harvard, Ernie Thayer had thought a lot about the question of what he might do with his life. What he *should* do, what his parents hoped and expected he'd do, as against what he *wanted* to do. Should he join the highly prosperous family business—a large firm of woolen mills in Worcester, among the region's most successful—eventually to become its president? Or should he follow his heart and become a writer? His experience at Harvard had pretty well convinced him that he had the talent, serving as editor of the school's humor magazine, *The Lampoon*, as well as contributing to its pages. More impressive, for two years he'd written the school's Hasty Pudding Club shows. More recently he'd spent a year and a half as a reporter and feature writer for the San Francisco *Examiner* (owned by the father of a Harvard classmate William Randolph Hearst).

During some eighteen happy months on the *Examiner*, up to February 1888, in addition to doing a regular stint of ordinary reporting, he contributed to the paper editorials, prose features, and even poetry, his light verse adding a pleasant touch to the paper's crowded columns. Whether it was his own idea or a policy of the paper's, he hadn't been given a by-line. The verse he always signed simply "Phin," a shortening of the nickname bestowed on him by his Harvard friends, Phinney (a schoolboy link to the first name of P.T. Barnum, Phineas). His essays and other prose pieces were either anonymous or carried his initials, E.L.T.

When he came home to Worcester early in 1888—to rest and recuperate from a spell of ill health, or so he later claimed—he'd kept up desultory writing for the *Examiner*, mailing contributions every week or so. At first, on leaving San Francisco, with plenty of time to think during the long train ride across the country, he'd felt no real doubt that he'd be returning to the coast to continue his career as a journalist. After he'd been home for a couple of weeks, however, nagging doubts had arisen. Now he had moments when he surprised himself by actually wondering if the writing life

Ernest L. Thayer as he looked in 1885, the year of his gradua-tion from Harvard. Three years later, after a stint on the San Francisco Examiner, *at his home in Worcester, Massachusetts, he wrote* Casey at the Bat.

was what he really wanted. His long stint of newspapering, he had to admit, had dulled more than a little his taste for the life of a working journalist. As he said, he'd discovered something he should have known, that writing on demand and under a deadline was a world away from the leisurely, self-serving composition he'd known in school. "Writing for a living," he confessed in a letter to his family, "is very different from running a college paper."

He'd even begun to question his literary abilities. During the heady days on the *Lampoon* he'd rated himself pretty high, at least in potential. Now he'd begun to realize that his talent might not rise much above the ordinary. He could turn out copy for the paper as it was needed, straight reporting, fact-pieces, think-pieces, editorials, light nonsense verse and humorous essays, even obituaries. But as he now began to understand, that only put him in a class with hundreds, even thousands of other writers on other papers across the country.

There was also the economic side. After getting his paycheck from the *Examiner* for those eighteen months he'd become very conscious that the writing business didn't pay very well. If he were involved in the family firm his income even to start would be ten times higher than it was with the *Examiner*. He wasn't sure that he was willing to suffer to *that* extent for his art.

But there was still another reason, which by itself would probably have been enough to explain all his hesitations: in San Francisco he'd fallen in love. Encouraged by the girl, he'd happily written home about marrying, and settling down on the coast. The young lady was the beautiful sister of a close friend and classmate, Eugene Lent. In the end, however, she changed her mind, and chose someone else, leaving young Thayer devastated. That happened in the late fall of 1887, the bad news coming as a total surprise. Within weeks he'd left San Francisco and was back in his parents home in Worcester. With the approach of spring three months later, he found, the pain hadn't eased.

The poem he'd begun writing that May about a town called Mudville, was as much an effort to forget Miss Lent as it was to produce still another bit of forgettable verse.

It was quite a timely little ballad he had in mind, meant to celebrate the craze over professional baseball that had within the last two or three years virtually swept the country. At the time, organized, big-league baseball was still new, barely a dozen years old (the amateur variety went back another forty or so years, well into pre-Civil War days.) The pro game, however, still had not reached all the way across the country—only as far as Chicago—and few expected it would *ever* find its way as far west as Los Angeles or San Francisco. The semi-pro and amateur brand was the best that West Coast fans could hope for on a regular basis. Only when one or more of the big-league teams, on finishing the regular season, went barnstorming around the country were West Coast "cranks" treated to the authentic professional variety.

As he once confessed, Thayer at first wasn't much of a baseball fan. In college he'd gotten caught up in the game— as a spectator, never a player—but mostly because his good friend and classmate, and *Lampoon* colleague, Sam Winslow, another Worcester boy, was the Harvard team captain and star player. For three years he'd hardly missed a Harvard home game, also attending many away. During 1885, his final year in school, the team, led by Winslow, had gone undefeated, taking the college championship. After graduation he'd spent some months making the grand tour of Europe before settling into his job at the *Examiner*. There he again got caught up in baseball, mostly because he was assigned to cover some of the California League games, a semi-pro outfit.

In one of his first reports—printed on December 27, 1887—he notes the galvanizing effect on West Coast fans produced by the arrival of a big-league team from the East, Louisville of the American Association. "Never before in the history of the national game," wrote Thayer, "has there been such excitement in baseball circles as has existed during the past two days. The meeting between the clubs of the California League and the Louisvilles has created a furor." When a California team, the Haverlys, actually beat the big leaguers, Frisco fans "found it difficult to restrain their enthusiasm."

Even without the professionals baseball fever was rampant among coast fans, who supported their local teams as ardently as fans supported those in New York, Detroit, Pittsburgh, Indianapolis, or Chicago. The California League, wrote Thayer that April

> . . . has inaugurated another season under the most auspicious circumstances. Yesterday the sphere was set in motion and the ash was wielded with a will, and ten thousand pairs of eyes gazed with enthusiasm on as interesting an exhibition on the

diamond field as has been witnessed for many a day . . .

The opening game was all that could be desired. It was beyond the anticipations of the most sanguine, and not even the bickering critic could find a flaw. The work on the diamond displayed the fact that since the close of last season the tossers [pitchers] have taken considerable practice . . .

It was November 1887 when coast fans, including Thayer, got their first look at the professional game's true celebrities, the big hitters, led by the formidable Roger Connor and the glamorous King Kelly. Both the Giants (with Kelly of Boston along as an added attraction), and the Louisville Browns had arrived in San Francisco and had taken the town by storm. When Connor in a game on December 4 played at the brand-new Haight Street stadium, not only hit the park's inaugural home-run, but blasted it clear out of the park over the right-field fence, Thayer was there. When King Kelly came up at a crucial moment in a game against the Frisco Pioneers, and struck out, Thayer was not only there, he captured the exciting incident for the *Examiner* in a passage that reads curiously like a preliminary sketch of the poem he would write five months later. The four-strike rule of 1887 was then still in effect, and at the plate, wrote Thayer, Kelly was greeted,

. . . with a generous burst of applause as he assumed his graceful attitude facing Lorrigan. None of the Giants were on the bench; they were standing up watching Lorrigan.

"One ball," cried Sheridan, then "One strike, two strikes, three strikes." The Beauty had not struck at the ball, and he was getting interested. The crowd encouraged Lorrigan to "Strike him out, Ed."

Lorrigan stood facing Kel for the final effort. In came the sphere, the Beauty made a lunge with his bat which met nothing but the air, and amidst the shouts of the crowd the "Only Mike" retired to the bench.

During his first year with the *Examiner*, Thayer had written only prose. Back in school he'd contributed an occasional poem to the *Lampoon*, none showing much true skill or originality, but only the usual college humor. In San Francisco, as he later explained, his interest in verse again was stirred when he came across a volume of W.S. Gilbert's *Bab Ballads*—and stirred even deeper when he read in the volume's Preface that the famous *Bab Ballads* had begun life as mere newspaper verse. All had, wrote Gilbert, "originally appeared in the columns of *FUN* when that periodical was under the editorship of the late Tom Hood." All had been written hastily and under the pressure "of having to turn out a quantity of lively verse by a certain day in every week." The literarily ambitious Thayer, too, was just then under the necessity of having to churn out copy, including light verse, by a certain day in every week, so Gilbert's famous example made an instant strong appeal to him. Comic ballads became his professional aim and his spare-time passion.

Light verse, often a bit too much on the silly side, the *Bab Ballads* were founded on grotesque exaggeration, trick-

THE "BAB" BALLADS.

MISTER WILLIAM.

O H, listen to the tale of MISTER WILLIAM, if you please,
  Whom naughty, naughty judges sent away beyond the
seas.
He forged a party's will, which caused anxiety and strife,
Resulting in his getting penal servitude for life.

1

Thayer's writing of humorous "ballads" for the Examiner, *with
Casey as the most memorable, was a direct result of his reading
of the* Bab Ballads *of W.S. Gilbert, librettist for Sir Arthur
Sullivan in such classic works as* Pinafore *and* The Mikado.

ily deft prosody, ridiculous names, and mad non-sequiturs of the Lewis Carroll kind. Captivated, young Thayer promptly and happily began to imitate the Englishman's style and approach, or as he later confessed, "decided I could do something in that line."

His efforts, unashamed imitations of Gilbert, were accepted, and for some three months, up to the time of his departure from San Francisco, he contributed a weekly "ballad" to the *Examiner*'s Sunday issue. The last of the series— no longer a mere imitation but something wonderfully fresh and new—would be *Casey at the Bat*.

One further curious fact must not be passed over: this same W.S. Gilbert, as librettist for the composer Sir Arthur Sullivan, also profoundly touched the career of DeWolf Hopper. Many of the songs sung by Hopper in operettas of the Eighties and Nineties were modeled on numbers in such Gilbert and Sullivan works as *The Mikado*, *Pinafore*, *Patience*, *The Yoeman of the Guard*, and others. From time to time Hopper also took leading roles in one or another Gilbert and Sullivan work playing the Broadway Theaters.

In a way, behind both of *Casey*'s two births, the writing of the ballad, and its public presentation, stands the merry, smiling figure of an exceedingly clever Englishman.

At the desk in his Chatham Street study, Thayer had made up his mind. He would center his new poem on the classic baseball situation, a moment of great tension and unfailing high drama. "I evolved Casey," he told an inter-

viewer, "from the situation I had seen so often in baseball—
a crack batsman coming to bat, with the bases filled, and
then falling down. Everyone well knows what immense
excitement there is when that situation occurs in baseball,
especially when one of the best batsmen of the team comes
up. The enthusiasm is at fever heat, and if the batsman
makes good the crowd goes wild; while if the batsman strikes
out, as Casey did, the reverse is the case, and the silence that
prevails is almost appalling."

The situation he describes did of course arise "often"
in games, it always caused intense excitement in the stands.
A search through the papers for even one month of the
1888 season turns up many instances. Here conveniently,
are a couple that occurred in the same game and involved
the day's two leading sluggers, Connor of New York and
Dan Brouthers of Detroit. In the Giants' fifth, some frantic
action had filled the bases, "so there was a great buzz of
excitement when Roger stepped to the plate, but a fearful
groan when he was called out on strikes. What hard luck
Roger is having of late!" In the ninth inning of the Detroit
game, Brouthers team was two runs behind when consecu-
tive hits put two men aboard:

> What a hub-bub there was at that. Nobody out
> and the tying run only ninety feet from home . . .
> now Brouthers stepped to the plate and every-
> body fidgeted. They were afraid of the big fellow.
> He made one of his wickedest whacks at the ball,
> and it shot from his bat like lightning toward
> third. Whitney [at third] jumped up, caught it,

touched third before Campau could get back, and it saved the day for New York.

Then a great cheer swept over the ground, and hundreds made a rush for Whitney to carry him off the field in triumph on their shoulders, but he was too quick for them and sprinted for the clubhouse.

Surely the slightly-built, thirty-year-old Art Whitney deserved those cheers—with his bare hands taking a shot off the explosive bat of the mighty Brouthers and turning it into a double play. Of course, in having *his* man go down swinging at empty air, Thayer was exactly right.

In his ballad, concluded Thayer, it will be the ninth inning. The featured team will be behind, say by two runs. On base will be two men, the tying runs, so that the next batter, if he hits a home run, will be the winning run. Accompanied by the thunderous shouts of the partisan crowd, up to bat comes the team's renowned slugger, a man whose timely, titanic hitting has repeatedly snatched victory from defeat. Cheered on by his imploring fans, the mighty man steps up to the plate, a threatening, lordly presence. Twice he declines to swing, disdainfully taking two called strikes.

Shall he be allowed once again to rescue his teammates and save the game by a colossal homer? That's what a reader will hope for and expect. Or, as mostly happens, both in baseball and in real life, should the hero be made to fail? Which ending would be most effective, in terms of the game, in terms of literature? Which would tell most about the players, about the fans, about baseball itself? The opening lines of the first stanza came easily:

> The outlook wasn't brilliant for the Mudville nine that day;
> The score stood four to two with but one inning more to play.
> And then when Cooney died at first, and Barrows did the same,
> A sickly silence fell upon the patrons of the game.

There! the youthful author thought contentedly as he sat back and re-read the four lines. He had it! The tone, the rhythm, the style, the detail, the situation all sounding just like a regular newspaper account of a game, but with the added charm of rhyme and rhythm. Importantly, it echoed the standard baseball phrasing, an effect for which he deliberately aimed. Such expressions as "died at first," and "patrons of the game," and "a sickly silence," show up repeatedly in the day's baseball coverage. The phrase "died at first"—meaning thrown out at first—was so familiar that it had a variant, "taken to the cemetery."

The low-key opening sounds a little high-flown—"The outlook wasn't brilliant"—but wording very like it shows up again and again on the sports pages. For instance: "the outlook was anything but encouraging" (NY *Times*, 7/25/88), "The out-look was not very promising" (NY *Times*, 8/10/88), "The outlook was bright" (NY *Times*, 6/13/88). For the word "brilliant" we have "Both sides played brilliant ball" (NY *Times*, 8/3/88); "the base-running was far from brilliant" (NY *World*, 9/20/88); and "the fielding was sharp and brilliant" (NY *Herald*, 7/3/88). To match "sickly silence" there is "The crowd was sick" (Chicago *Tribune*,

8/16/88), and "a sickening thud of silence" (NY *Herald*, 7/8/88).

As he continued to write, Thayer deftly built into his lines those small, evocative phrases, so familiar to the day's baseball fans. In the poem there are some thirty of them, and no doubt a close match for every one would turn up with a reading of the papers for a full season. They may have been dragged up from memory as he wrote. More likely, he first went through the back files of newspapers picking up phrases he felt might be useful.*

This is not to say that the poem is unoriginal. In the sensitive way he selected and arranged his materials, Thayer demonstrated the touch of a true artist, achieving a clever mosaic of sound and sense. His control of diction, for instance, and subtle nuance, is particularly fine. With the accomplishment of that first stanza, he needed only to continue thinking himself a reporter writing up an important game, heightening the fun and sharpening the drama with a little deft shading here and there.

Then he went further and with a few little verbal twists he created a mock-serious air, nicely burlesqueing the writers themselves, the professional baseball scribes of the Eighties.

If, as he wrote, Thayer pictured in his mind any particular real-life player in the part of Casey, he never said. He did deny that the precise character of the slugger, and the poem itself, had an actual model or inspiration, and no doubt this was the truth. Yet it meant only that the poem hadn't been generated or inspired by any specific incident or player. It

---

*See Appendix B for more on Thayer's phrasing.

doesn't preclude the likelihood that the figure of Casey as a representative of all the game's mighty hitters may derive from or reflect one or more of the day's prominent batsmen. If so, two of them are far and away the most likely, the two that Thayer knew best. The mighty Casey, it can safely be concluded, was a combination of Roger Connor and King Kelly, of Connor's tremendous power and imposing presence, and Kelly's winning ways and crowd appeal, his uncanny ability to come through in the clutch.

It can be no accident that Thayer had for the first time seen both men in action, up close in California, only months before beginning his poem, both performing in front of ecstatic crowds of adoring fans.

Connor's fitness all by himself for the role is inescapable. For fans of the 1880's he would have been entirely sufficient as a real life model for the mighty Casey. Perhaps he lacked something of that debonaire quality displayed by Casey when he "lightly doffed his cap" (Kelly was a great one for cap-tipping, needing some way of acknowledging the constant attention of the crowd), or when "with haughty grandeur" he ignored the speeding ball and took a strike. That sort of theater was more in Kelly's line, the only nineteenth-century player whose stature could be said to match that of Babe Ruth. Like Ruth also he was a genuinely likeable personality, friendly to all who approached him, greatly admired and liked even by his opponents. His reputation as a drinker he never denied, he never tried to hide it, and people accepted without difficulty that aspect of his life as part of the Kelly image.

Perhaps the best indication of Kelly's hold on the pop-

Michael J. "King" Kelly. For a dozen years he blazed through organized baseball, its most daring base-runner and the 19th century's greatest all-round talent. In 1888, with Boston, he was at his zenith, baseball's first celebrity-superstar.

The feared Roger Conner, New York Giants first baseman and leading long-distance slugger of the 19th century. Thayer watched him in action some months before writing Casey.

ular mind was the song that celebrated his most electrifying talent, that of base-runner. "Slide, Kelly, Slide!" was sung in music halls, bars, and private homes throughout the Eighties and Nineties. It was in fact one of the earliest phonograph records available to the buying public, in the form of a wax cylinder. For years it was also a board game found in many parlors.

But Kelly must not be thought of only as a glamorous personality. He was one of the truly great players in baseball history, an all-round marvel. Every year for over a decade he was near the top in each of a dozen offensive categories—three times batting champion, once with .388—and led all as a base-runner and as a defensive innovator. By those who know, he is still talked of as the most completely gifted all-round talent ever to take the field. His only competition, as an all-arounder, would perhaps come from Honus Wagner and Willie Mays, but neither of these had Kelly's lightning quick, imaginative, daring approach to the game. Fred Pfeffer, who played alongside the King in some thousand games at Chicago, was awed by him:

> . . . he was a creator. His strongest point was that he was always ready—he could take advantage of a misplay which others couldn't see until afterwards . . . I have seen him make plays that others never dreamed possible, and many things he did with the Chicagos have never been duplicated . . . batting, fielding, baserunning, quickness, decision, and judgment, he was the peer of them all. He played not by rules or instruction but by

instinct . . . to him belonged that degree of per-
fection, that faculty known as baseball sense. I
never knew Kel to hesitate in a close play. Before
the play came up he seemed to have anticipated
it . . .

A perfect illustration of what Pfeffer called "plays that
others never dreamed possible" occurred in a game against
Chicago in 1885, in which Kelly attempted something that
no player, apparently, had ever tried before, an outright steal
of home. It was the ninth inning, his team was one run
behind, and Kelly was on third, having doubled then stolen
a base. As the pitcher wound up, to the astonishment of
everyone in the ballpark, Kelly broke from third and went
streaking for the plate. Down he went in a desperate slide,
there was a collision at home with the catcher—who a split
second before had caught the pitched ball—and in a cloud of
dust, as the crowd roared its excitement, the catcher and
Kelly, both prostrate, looked up at the umpire. To the loud
disgust of the fans he called Kelly out. But it was close, and
before Kelly the feat had seemed foolhardy, a virtual impos-
sibility. From then on stealing home was a feature of the
game, not common, but tremendously exciting when it did
happen. Who may have been first to do it successfully isn't
known. It may have been Kelly himself.

Some of the antics attributed to Kelly as marking his
personal style of play actually were staples of the game at the
time. Kelly simply tried and got away with them more often.
The best example was his trick of "cutting bases," or "cutting angles," when trying to score from second. If the

umpire's attention was momentarily elsewhere—at that time there was only one umpire—he'd veer sharply toward home, missing the bag at third by five or ten feet. "His policy has always been the scoring of runs," complained *The Clipper* in February 1887, "whether honestly or not. He has on more than one occasion run from second-base to the home-plate without touching the third base," in this way sometimes delivering the winning run. But this particular bit of ungentlemanly—and illegal—conduct was fairly common then, and was hugely enjoyed by the fans, those at least rooting for the runner's team. Nor was it so easy to pull off. Here's what happened to another Boston player, Dick Johnston, when he attempted it in a game of August 1888. The tongue-in-cheek description in the *Herald*'s story shows how casually the infraction was viewed:

> "Ray slammed a whistling grounder down to Richardson, which Danny failed to hold. Johnston started for home but in his enthusiasm neglected the important ceremony of touching third base. In fact he gouged off a large slice of territory from that part of the diamond. Umpire Valentine saw the act and howled out a warning. Dicky, with great presence of mind, fled back to the haven of refuge where he stood like a graven image."

In another way Kelly anticipated Babe Ruth, when he was sold by the Chicago White Stockings to Boston. The price was an unbelievable $10,000, a sale and a price that rocked the baseball world every bit as much as did the sale of Ruth by Boston to the Yankees forty years later. From then on Kelly was known to press and public as "the Ten-thousand Dollar Beauty." The curious title was borrowed from a young actress of the time, Louise Montague, who supposedly had been awarded that sum in winning a beauty contest. Sportswriters found the same tag just right for their favorite baseball star.

Even as Thayer was picturing the great Casey in his ballad, he was or could have been reading in the papers about some fresh Kelly exploits. He wrote his poem, as he said, sometime in May 1888, and it was on April 30, and May 1-3, that Boston, led by the King, played its four-game series against the Giants at the Polo Grounds. The Boston *Globe*, certainly read by Thayer, featured Boston's two wins, in both of which Kelly starred—running wild in the first—and in one of the losses, in which Kelly's two-run homer almost saved the day. Of course, in those same four games Thayer also had the impressive example of Roger Connor to draw on, no home runs but several exciting long distance blasts that were caught, and three triples.

Kelly and Connor on the same field, the pair coming to bat a total of thirty-four times in the wild, four-game series, and it all happened just as Thayer was picturing the Mudville fans praying that their hero would "get a whack at that." Here, surely, at a ball park in teeming Manhattan during four days in the spring of 1888, was the real-life background of the mighty Casey's story.

Suddenly Thayer knew how his poem must end. To capture the soul of baseball he must portray, lovingly exag-gerated, the devastating effect of failure on keyed-up fans in

A famous painting of King Kelly (detail) doing what he did better than anyone—running the bases. Done in 1889 by artist Frank O. Small, it immortalizes the cry of "Slide, Kelly, slide!" that was often thundered from the stands by excited crowds. Here he goes into second base head first. More often he used a hook slide, a technique her personally perfected, if he didn't invent it.

The Boston team of 1890. King Kelly sits at Manager Hart's left. Dan Brouthers is 3rd from right, rear. Two great pitchers, Hoss Radbourne and John Clarkson are seated 2nd and 3rd from left.

a crucial situation. This once, the celebrated hometown hero must flop.

For such an ending it would hardly be fair to use Kelly's name, or Connor's, or any other known ballplayer. With that there popped into Thayer's head another Irish name, one out of his own past. In high school, once, a "big, dour, Irish lad," as Thayer described him, named Dan Casey, had resented something that the slightly-built Thayer had said or written about him. At their next meeting the offended Casey made his feelings known, "his big, clenched, red hands white at the knuckles." Thayer escaped any harm from the high-school Casey, but couldn't resist tagging his failed slugger with the name.

The lines of the poem, as Thayer continued to write, now came easily, being hardly more than a description, with little touches added, of sights and sounds he'd many times heard or seen on the ball field, or read about in the papers. The sixth stanza, bringing the confident Casey up to the bat, would have fitted well with either Connor or Kelly, but perhaps best with the King:

There was ease in Casey's manner as he stepped into his place;
There was pride in Casey's bearing and a smile on Casey's face.
And when, responding to the cheers, he lightly doffed his hat,
No stranger in the crowd could doubt 'twas Casey at the bat.

Again, as Thayer went on, the poem gained in authenticity, and a kind of familiar charm, when Thayer deftly built in phrases found in the daily accounts of games in the papers (a little too much given to rhetorical flights and literary flourishes, these accounts were as full and detailed in describing the action on the field as anything written today). For the worried Mudville spectators there is "stricken multitude." For the ball itself there is "leather-covered sphere" and "spheroid"—*every* baseball story then, it seems, had one or both of these!

There were "sturdy batsman," and an old standby, "tore the cover off the ball," and the evocative "rising tumult." There was Casey pounding "with cruel violence" his bat on the plate, exaggerated language but for this determined action just right. The tenth stanza, implying that the entire scene, the fast-developing drama, was being controlled by the larger-than-life Casey, sets the stage perfectly. The word "stilled" in the second line, and "ignored" in the last, are both just right:

> With a smile of Christian charity great Casey's visage shone;
> He stilled the rising tumult, he bade the game go on;
> He signaled to the pitcher, and once more the spheroid flew;
> But Casey still ignored it, and the umpire said, "Strike two."

It is in the final four stanzas, perfectly echoing—but taken just a notch higher—the elevated language and feel of the day's newspaper coverage, that Thayer's art is most in evidence. Stanzas eleven and twelve—preparing for the wonderful close of the thirteenth—tighten the drama as expertly as any modern playwright:

> "Fraud!" cried the maddened thousands, and echo answered fraud;
> But one scornful look from Casey and the audience was awed.

They saw his face grow stern and cold, they saw his muscles strain,
And they knew that Casey wouldn't let that ball go by again.

The sneer is gone from Casey's lip, his teeth are clenched in hate;
He pounds with cruel violence his bat upon the plate.
And now the pitcher holds the ball, and now he lets it go,
And now the air is shattered by the force of Casey's blow.

No furious crowd ever shouted the single word "Fraud!" in unison to protest an umpire's call (a variety of saltier oaths is preferred!). No batter, mighty or otherwise, ever awed into silence a stadium full of hysterical fans by "one scornful look." Casey does so, and the reader too is awed, but only because of Thayer's art. That simple, threefold repetition, "And now . . . and now . . . and now," advancing the action a notch at a time, is the best example of his mastery.

A final stanza was added telling the result of Casey's air-shattering blow. Thayer then tacked on what seems to be a curiously whimsical subtitle: "A Ballad of the Republic, Sung in the Year 1888."

Why "of the Republic'? Why not "of Baseball"?

Why "Sung"? It was not a song, but a poem, without music.

Why specify the year? What did 1888 have to do with anything?

The readiest answer to all those questions is probably the correct one. While writing his poem, if not before, he'd come to realize how much a part of the fabric of American life baseball had become, both amateur and professional (the previous September in San Francisco in an *Examiner* piece he'd written: "There is no doubt that the dear old familiar game of baseball is an enchanting pastime, and has a firm grasp on the popular mind. There is something fascinating about the sport that defies resistance, even from dignified and patriarchal members of the bench and bar"). In that sub-title he was recording and celebrating that fact. His plain, simple little ballad, he was subtly declaring, was about much more than one special moment in a game, a pastime. It also uncovered something about American life ("the Republic"), something deep down in the American character. Then, having given his hint, he was clever enough to let it go at that. His poem would say the rest, at least for those able to read, not between, but behind the lines. "Sung in the Year 1888" was his quietly exuberant way both of characterizing and dating his discovery. If any year in baseball history is to be picked as the crucial one, the historical pivot, then it's 1888. In that year, baseball still hovered on a line between the old and the new, between birth and maturity. It had become pretty much what it is today, yet hadn't entirely lost the fresh, boyish air of its rowdy beginnings, its note of *abandon*.

As to what Thayer had accomplished in those thirteen masterful stanzas, let the man who knew the poem better than anyone ever has, better perhaps than even its author, give his opinion of its unique excellence. DeWolf Hopper, after he'd been performing it for some thirty years, wrote that Thayer's ballad:

. . . is as perfect an epiphany of our national game today as it was when every player drank his coffee from a moustache cup. There are one or more Caseys in every league, bush or big, and there is no day in the playing season that this same supreme tragedy, as stark as Aristophanes for the moment, does not befall on some field.

It is unique in all verse in that it is not only funny and ironic, but excitingly dramatic, with the suspense built up to a perfect climax. There is no lame line among the fifty-two. And so, although it might be thought I should have had my fill of Casey, I hope to go to bat with him for many more seasons before we both strike out . . .

He did, of course, go to bat again with his old friend, in fact continued to step up to the plate for a whole decade, until his death in 1935, never slackening in his praise or the intensity of his recital.

Neatly writing out the finished poem, Thayer added in the lower right-hand corner his usual pseudonym, "Phin." For not using his real name there was no particular reason, pen-names then being a mere affectation, carried over from an earlier, more formal time. He then made a copy for himself, put the thin manuscript in an envelope, and addressed it to the *Examiner*, San Francisco. Dropping it into the local post-box, he turned his mind to other, more pressing matters.

Not the least curious part of the story is the fact that, while *Casey* takes on a life of its own, Thayer as author now fades out of the picture, not to be heard of again in connection with his poem for almost twenty years.

3

WALLACK'S THEATER, MAY 1888
THE LADY OR THE TIGER?

URTAIN TIME AT WALLACK'S THEATER EACH EVENING—SIX
days a week with a matinee at two on Saturdays—was
eight o'clock, facts stated in all the ads. Also prominent
in the ads was an announcement as to the theater's air-con-
ditioned comfort, anticipating the summer heat: "cooled by
tons of ice," stored in the basement from where the frigid air
was wafted up into the hall. On May 7, 1888, well before
curtain-time, everyone of the house's nine-hundred-plus seats
was filled. Muted strains of melody from the twenty-two-
piece orchestra in the pit before the stage entertained the
patiently waiting audience.

In part, the full house was a result of its being a first
night, and also word-of-mouth anticipation sparked by some
clever advance publicity. A master at grabbing free space, the
company's owner-director, Col. John McCaull (the title was
legitimate: he'd been an officer with the Confederate force,

Mosby's rangers, in the Civil War), weeks before the opening and managed to capture a good deal of it in most New York papers. Two interviews appeared in the New York *Times*, at the beginning and end of April. The experienced impressario knew just what to say.

"I never read a libretto which struck me as so good as that of *The Lady or the Tiger*," sweepingly declared McCaull to the attentive *Times* reporter. With a look of utter sincerity he added, "I have submitted this work to other good judges and their opinion agrees with mine, that Sydney Rosenfeld has produced the best book for a comic opera that has ever been placed before the public in this or any other country." Quite simply, this latest production of the McCaull company was far and away "the finest work he had staged during his twenty years in the theater."

Dutifully the *Times* reporter wrote it all down just as it was spoken, and was about to resume asking questions when McCaull, without any urging, went on.

"DeWolf Hopper is so delighted with his part," he declared, "that he is counting the days which will elapse before he can sing it. When you find a comedian praising instead of condemning a character he is cast to play, you may be sure there is merit in the part." With *Tiger* on the boards, insisted the Colonel, the coming Broadway season "will be the most brilliant that has ever been given in this city." All the scenes of the new play "will be historically correct, as well as executed in as fine a manner as Mr. Goetscher's brush is capable of doing them."

The captivating plot, he explained, "is laid in the year 479 B.C., and the authorities have been ransacked and historical experts catechised in order to secure exact reproductions of the Greek architecture of the period . . . with regard to the costumes . . . the people on stage will be dressed in the same manner and so far as possible in the same material as the citizens' of old Greece . . . the large chorus is being drilled by constant rehearsals."

On the sidewalk in front of the theater, capturing the attention of the hurrying passersby, stood a large poster showing the play's hapless lover flanked by a ferocious tiger and a beautiful maiden. To his eye, ventured the *Times* reporter, the poster seemed to tip the answer to the question in the play's title, made it look as if "it would be the tiger" that the unlucky lover would find himself facing, rather than the maiden.

Is that the answer, pressed the reporter. Come on Colonel, is it to be the tiger? You can trust me. I won't print it. Just between us . . .

"A fine painting, isn't it?" responded McCaull, avoiding the question. "We're preserving absolute secrecy on that score, a kind of Gilbert-and-Sullivan secrecy, so I really can't . . ."

The question as to the lady or the tiger, he added, has provoked an extraordinary amount of argument, ever since the story's initial publication some six years before in the popular *Century*. "It has even been a theme for discussion at debating societies in England as well as this country. Now as Mr. Rosenfeld undertakes to settle this question, it would not be fair to give it away before the first night at Wallack's."

Smilingly he finished, "You will find the libretto, however, in the safe, if you know the combination!"

Colonel John A. McCaull, owner-manager of New York's leading light opera company in which DeWolf Hopper starred. McCaull's eager agreement to having a "Baseball Night" at the theater made possible the debut of Casey in August 1888.

Right: Newspaper ads for Hopper's The Lady or the Tiger? at Wallack's Theater shortly after it opened in May 1888. Hopper had not yet achieved the top spot in comic opera that he would reach and hold for thirty years.

AMUSEMENTS.

A.—WALLACK TESTIMONIAL.

MR. AUGUSTIN DALY AND Mr. A. M. PALMER
beg to announce that
THE SALE OF PRIVATE BOXES
(34 in number, seating six persons each)
for the TESTIMONIAL PERFORMANCE of
HAMLET
IN HONOR OF LESTER WALLACK
at the Metropolitan Opera House, May 21, 1888,
will take place at
THE MADISON SQUARE THEATER,

TO-DAY—TUESDAY, MAY [illegible]—TO-DAY

AT 4 O'CLOCK P. M.

UPSET PRICE OF ALL BOXES $60 EACH.
SALE BY MR. JOHN H. DRAPER.

WALLACK'S.
Under the direction of Mr. HENRY E. ABBEY.
TO-NIGHT, AT 8 O'CLOCK,

McCAULL OPERA CO.

JOHN A. McCAULL, Sole Proprietor and Manager

THE LADY - - OR - - THE TIGER.

By SYDNEY ROSENFELD.
Music by Julius J. Lyons and Adolph Nowak.
GENERAL ADMISSION 50c. MATINEE SATURDAY. Seats secured two weeks in advance.

CASINO. BROADWAY AND 39TH ST.
Evenings at 8. Matinée Saturday at 2.
A MOST REMARKABLE SUCCESS.
HOUSES CROWDED.
OVER 750 PERFORMANCES.
POSITIVELY LAST WEEK OF THE GREATEST COMIC OPERA EVER PRESENTED,
"ERMINIE."
GREETED WITH SHOUTS OF LAUGHTER.
Admission, 50c.; balcony, $1; orchestra, $1 50.
MONDAY, MAY 14, the Hungarian operetta,
NADJY.
By FRANÇOIS CHASSAIGNE, composer of Falka.
Entirely new costumes, scenery, appointments, &c.
Seats can now be secured.

AMPHION. BEDFORD AV.,
BROOKLYN

One week only, May 14 to 19,

BOOTH AND BARRETT.

[illegible]—Julius Caesar, Macbeth, Hamlet, [illegible]

Promptly at eight o'clock in Wallack's large hall there sounded the brassy blare of French horns and trumpets, the clash of cymbols, and the deep-toned rolling of kettle drums, and slowly the tall, wide curtain parted to reveal a street in fifth-century Greece busy with hurrying people. For the next two and a half hours the hall was filled with tuneful songs, comic or sentimental, and with gales of laughter, a large part of it generated by the antics of DeWolf Hopper as the King. In the second act came his show-stopper, a long, catchy number in which he comments not only on the play's action but on a variety of New York City's and the country's problems. Titled for its refrain, "I'm On Very Good Terms With Myself," it brought down the house.

The final act was set in a circular arena with two doors opening onto it. In the middle, facing the doors, stands the perplexed lover agonizing over his decision as to which door to choose, and wondering what to do if a tiger comes bounding out. Then, visible in the stands, he spots his love, the King's daughter. Cleverly she signals for him to choose the right-hand door, which he unhesitatingly proceeds to do. As the door swings open the cringing lover sees neither the lady nor the tiger. Instead, beaming coyly, out steps a fat, old woman. The King's daughter by bribery has managed to substitute for the beautiful maiden her own compliant servant.

Turning to the King, the relieved lover argues that since he was promised a beautiful maiden but didn't get one, and took the chance of being eaten alive, he has successfully passed the ordeal and should be set free. The King agrees, and then goes further and gives the lover his daughter's hand.

The audience loved it, and to resounding waves of applause the curtain falls.

The notices, however, most of them, weren't good. The *Evening Post* found the libretto "very wearisome," and thought the music "not above mediocrity . . . it is nearly all reminiscent." The female lead, Catarina Marco, an opera diva brought all the way from Italy for the role, the *Post* saw as "hardly equal to her part; she was often false in her tone, and her voice has a disagreeable vibratto."

The *Times*, too, found the Rosenfeld libretto wanting, though it thought it did offer "a very amusing solution to Mr. Stockton's problem." The musical score, while it had two or three good numbers, regrettably proved to be "less brilliant than had been expected." Disappointingly, the imported Miss Marco "has evidently seen her best days . . . her voice is much worn and she has a tremolo of heroic proportions." Still, concluded the *Times*, there was enough that was good in the operetta "to keep it on the stage for some time."

Reaping the most praise was DeWolf Hopper, really unstinted. "As Pausanias, the King," said the *Times*, "Hopper scored one of the greatest hits of his career. He was extraordinarily funny from beginning to end, and in some of the scenes he fairly surpassed any of his previous efforts." Still more explicit on Hopper's comic genius was the New York *Times*. Without him, declared the paper, the show would have collapsed: "What a King Sparta had when DeWolf Hopper held the throne against all comers! Surely never more rollicking, big-voiced, all-pervading, fun-loving, laughter-provoking ruler held a scepter . . . without such an interpreter, illustrator, and expounder, endowed with the richest stores of genuine humor, much of Mr. Rosenfeld's efforts to amuse would have fallen flat."

The Spartan court was kept "all astir," and no one in the audience allowed attention to wander or flag "while Hopper was on the stage."

It was Hopper's performance, in fact, and that of Mathilda Cottrelly as the Queen, that kept the play alive long enough for it to gather an audience and become at least a minor hit. Late in its third week, after some extensive tinkering—poor Signorina Marco and her annoying vibratto were among the first to go—it began playing to near-capacity houses. Then, to the surprise of composer and critics alike, many of its songs found a public and soon "were being whistled on the streets."

For Hopper's big number, "I'm On Very Good Terms With Myself," Rosenfeld kept supplying fresh new verses to catch the interest in topics current around the city. For any groups, large or small, that attended the show as a body, and informed the theater in advance, he'd write verses making a special appeal to that group. When a large contingent of the city's horse-racing fraternity announced that it would attend *The Lady or the Tiger?* as part of its annual celebration, Rosenfeld was ready. That night, Hopper's show-stopper included a racing verse. There may have been more but this is the only one that has survived:

When you get a straight tip on a horse that will win,
And you go to the track and you wager your tin,
Your face wears a satisfied, jubilant grin,

And you're on very good terms with yourself.
But oh, when it's run, and that horse, don't you see,
Who was such a sure thing, comes in, oh, dear me,
With his head, darn his skin, where his tail ought to be,
Then you're *not* on good terms with yourself!

McCaull, Hopper, Rosenfeld, the two composers, and the entire cast settled contentedly down for what looked like being a good run. Two or three months, anyway.

The Decoration Day doubleheader at the Polo Grounds always drew a huge crowd. Many fans who otherwise attended few Giant games during the year showed up on Decoration Day looking for excitement. The 1888 doubleheader, played on May 30, brought one of the largest crowds yet—some 18,000—creating an overflow problem that was accommodated in the usual way.

In a loop across the furthest part of the outfield, from right field all the way around to left field, a rope was strung. In this marked-off swathe of ground along the outfield edge fans were allowed to stand and view the game (much as today with golf where large crowds ring the course). The practice cut down the outfield distances by twenty or thirty feet, depending where the ropes were placed, making hits, especially home runs, that much easier. But since it was the same for both teams nobody complained. What else could you do? You couldn't turn fans away because the regular stands—curving around home plate from first base to third, leaving the remainder of the field's perimeter enclosed only by a ten-foot-high fence—were filled. Especially not at fifty cents a head and room for a couple of thousand standees! Packed in behind the rope they "formed a horseshoe around the playing lines and took a sun bath . . . they yelled, jumped around like colts, clapped hands, and threw their hats in the air . . . and enjoyed themselves hugely."

The Giants' opponent for the two games was Pittsburgh, a good team but just then mired in sixth place in the league standings. The New Yorks were expected to take both games handily.

By now, *The Lady or the Tiger?* had been running for a solid three weeks, and apparently was established (so much for the know-it-all reviewers!). Some twenty thousand satisfied customers had already paid to see it—tickets started at the usual fifty cents and rose to a dollar and a half for the best seats—a fact reported by the papers, and advance sales were holding strong. Hopper, now billed as the show's premier star and mainstay, had decided to reward himself by joining the festive Decoration Day crowd at the Polo Grounds and cheering his good friends on to victory. At the moment the Giants were in fourth place, seven games behind the leader, Chicago, with the next three teams closely bunched: Detroit, Boston, and New York. The season was still young, though, and all agreed that the Giants had as good a shot at the title as anyone.

Hopper's usual baseball chum, Digby Bell, was away in Philadelphia, singing in another McCaull group, so he went up to the park alone.

The first game, in the morning, was as expected a Giants win, in fact it was a route, 11 to 1. Its feature was a titanic home run by Roger Connor to the farthest part of center field. The afternoon game, however, brought a shock when Pittsburgh outhit New York for a surprisingly easy 8 to 4 victory.

On the Giants schedule for this home stand, before they left town for a swing through the midwest, were another ten games at the Polo Grounds. Whether Hopper attended any of them can't be said, but since they included several against the league leaders, Chicago, he probably managed one or two. If he was able to get uptown for the game on June 8th he would have witnessed a satisfying and impressive display by the Giants batters. Hitting five home runs in a total of twenty-four hits, they crushed Chicago by 19 to 2.

Chicago had begun the game in lighthearted fashion when its players marched onto the field attired in black dress-coats over their white baseball uniforms—the fancy, swallow-tail variety—and top hats, denoting their status as the prior year's champions, and current leaders. The ploy had tickled the crowd and it responded with a generous round of applause. After the devastating loss the swallow-tail coats and silk toppers were nowhere to be seen.

Chicago, however, had quickly gotten its revenge, walloping New York in the next three games straight. While all three games were hard-fought, the one played on June 8th provided the most excitement. Particularly there was one sparkling play by the Chicago left-fielder, Duke Farrell, in which he robbed Connor of a three-run homer:

> . . . it looked as though New York would surely tie the score in the eighth inning when . . . Tiernan hunted the ball safe for a single, then got

second on Daly's dropped ball, and was advanced to third on Ward's bunt, which gave him [Ward] first. The excitement was great, and with only one man out and the heavy hitters coming in it seemed certain that New York would tie or pass Chicago. But Connor's long fly was captured by Farrell, who threw to Daly [at the plate], catching Tiernan just off the home base. Terrific cheers greeted the young player . . .

Farrell's running catch of Connor's long, high blast, said the *Tribune*, was a wonder, and it was followed almost in the same motion by "his magnificent throw to the plate" to nail Tiernan racing in from third. (Shades of "The Catch" by Willie Mays!)

The final game in that series against Chicago produced several instances of the by-now familiar situation celebrated in Thayer's poem. Three times the Giants had the bases filled but couldn't score, batters going down on strikes one after the other: "Time and again men were on third, second, and first bases, and the outlook was bright. On three occasions all three bases were occupied by New York men, and a hit would have been of great value, but it never came."

"The outlook was bright," wrote this scribe in describing an actual game. "The outlook wasn't brilliant," wrote Thayer in the negative for his imaginary contest, but sounding just like the *Herald* reporter.

By early June attendance at Wallack's for *Tiger* had begun to drop slightly and the experienced McCaull saw that the end was in sight. By the middle of the month he'd decided to close it after another two weeks. He would then give his company a short holiday, and in mid-July would re-open with a revival of a Johann Strauss operetta he'd first given five years before, *Prince Methusalem*. Shrewdly guessing that Tiger's initial success wouldn't carry it past forty or fifty performances, he'd had *Methusalem* in rehearsal for some weeks. It would make the perfect vehicle, he thought, for his rising young star, the very tall, very funny, mellow-voiced DeWolf Hopper.

All these arrangements the *Times* thought newsworthy, including the destination of each of the vacationers. "The members of the McCaull Opera Company," it reported, "have already begun to scatter in all directions to enjoy their two weeks vacation. Col. McCaull . . . intends spending a few days with Lester Wallack in Stamford. DeWolf Hopper and his wife have already joined Miss Georgia Cayvan and her party on the Sound near Stamford. Mr. and Mrs. Digby Bell have gone to Block Island. . . . Col. Stevens will spend his Vacation in the foyer of Wallack's Theater taking orders for the opening night of *Prince Methusalem* . . ."

On a street in San Francisco, on June 8, 1888, a man stopped at a news stand to pick up his usual copy of the *Examiner*. Sometime during that day or evening he sat down to read it. When he reached page four he found a long poem—it filled almost an entire column from top to bottom—entitled *Casey at the Bat*. As his eyes ran along the rhythmic lines he smiled. When he finished, a broad grin brightened his heavy features.

The Chicago White Stockings pose at the Polo Grounds on June 8, 1888, with DeWolf Hopper (seated right front in gray suit) and DeWolf Bell (with cane at Hopper's right). The players are wearing tuxedos (clawhammer dress coats) over their uniforms as a joking way of displaying their status as 1887 champions. Cap Anson stands at rear, second from right.

A baseball fan for many years, he hugely enjoyed the way the lilting phrases evoked one of the game's high moments, chuckled to see how cleverly the poem ended, showing the hero baffled and defeated instead of winning the game with a towering home run.

After a moment's hesitation he reached into the drawer for a pair of scissors and clipped out the long narrow column containing the sprightly verses. Again he read them through, again grinned in delight. Then he casually dropped the slip of paper into the desk drawer.

The man was Arch Gunter, a leading novelist-playwright of the Eighties (Archibald Clavering Gunter was the name spread on his books and plays). In fact at this instant A.C. Gunter was the best-known, most successful writer on the American scene, his name known to more readers than that of Mark Twain. His first novel, *Mr. Barnes of New York*, had become a surprise sensation (a wealthy, brash young American goes adventuring in Europe), becoming a best seller in both England and the States, and in translation in much of Europe. Urged by several producers and theater managers, he was now in the process of turning the novel into a play, slated for Broadway production in October.

At present, sadly, but with good reason, Gunter is entirely forgotten, as are all his works. As an author he was on a par with today's writers who supply the unending flood of mass-market paperbacks and best-selling romance novels. His three dozen novels were all cut from the same common cloth: three hundred-page, small format books bound in yellow paper and selling for fifty cents. Superficial in plot, style, and character, naive in dialogue, they cleverly offered sexual

Casey at the Bat *as it appeared on page 4 of the San Francisco* Examiner, *Sunday, June 3, 1888. Next to it on the right is the weekly column of the well-know author Ambose Bierce. For an enlargement of this printing of Casey, see the Appendix.*

innuendo in the detailed descriptions of idealized young beauties, their clothes, and the enticing figures underneath, lovingly detailed. In that day the approach was new, and it clicked beyond Gunter's wildest hopes. Promptly he decided to be his own publisher, setting up the Home Publishing Company with offices on New York's Union Square at 14th Street, run by his wife.

Born in England in 1847, Gunter came to California with his family at age five, and was raised in San Francisco, where he later worked as a mining engineer. By 1879, after gaining some attention on the West Coast as a playwright, he moved east to New York and soon became a permanent resident. He continued writing plays, and in one of them, a little surprisingly, Richard Mansfield scored his first real triumph. With the success of *Mr. Barnes* he turned exclusively to novel-writing and during the ensuing decade churned them out one after another.

In June 1888, laden with fame and fortune, he'd gone back to San Francisco to pay a nostalgic visit to his parents and friends and his old home. He remained about a month, and by mid-July had returned to New York City to complete his task of turning *Mr. Barnes* into a play. In his wallet he carried the *Examiner* clipping, which he now and then took out to share with some of his baseball friends. Among those friends was a theatrical colleague, Col. John A. McCaull.

4

INTERLUDE: STROLLING THE RIALTO

NAT GOODWIN? ANY NEW YORKER IN THE 1880S COULD tell you who Nat Goodwin was. Anyone who went to the theater or read the papers.

One of the day's most admired actors, close friend of Hopper and Bell, Goodwin was also a personality known all up and down Broadway. To accompany him on one of his frequent strolls along the storied thoroughfare, especially the section known as the Rialto, is to enter the show-business world in which Casey will make his debut in mid-August of 1888.

In and out of the theater Goodwin could boast of having many friendships. But none, as he admitted, was more gratifying to him than that "between Digby Bell, DeWolf Hopper, and myself." All three had begun their careers in the Seventies, he explained, "at about the same time, and we have appeared often in the same characterizations, principally in comic and light opera, and each has enjoyed the others' performances more than his own."

Once, a few years later, Goodwin paused long enough
to set down a description of the Broadway he'd known and
worked on and loved in the Eighties. Especially for one mile-
long stretch of it he felt a deep nostalgia, a feeling no doubt
experienced equally by all the day's old stage troupers.
Covering some twenty blocks, it ran north from the theater
district at Union Square to another cluster of theaters on 34th
Street. For stage folk that glittering section of Broadway had
a particular name all its own, borrowed from Shakespeare's
Merchant of Venice, and now largely forgotten: The Rialto.

Goodwin's fond and careful memory of the storied
stretch (shortened here) affords an unusual, close-up view of
a vanished tradition of the New York theater world. Most of
the well-known names he mentions as meeting along the
Rialto, much celebrated then, have been cruelly obscured by
time. A few of them, pitifully few, still ring a bell:

> . . . what wouldn't I give to swing hack in time, to
> stroll down Broadway when all was congested and
> chaotic, but nevertheless a delightful potpourri of
> brilliance, genius, talent, and beauty . . . to stop
> and talk with the austere but charming Barney
> Macauley, to be joined by Charley Read, the
> delightful minstrel, the tall and always well-
> groomed Charles Thorne . . . clever George Knight,
> Billy Barr, Sol Russell, and John Drew!
>
> As you continue down, the distinguished
> members of Wallack's and the Union Square
> Theaters nod recognition. Then you return to the
> St. James Hotel to be met graciously by its popular

proprietor Billy Connors, fascinating Henry Perry, the wit of Broadway, and divers other men-about-town including the well-turned-out John Daly.

The gambler John Daly? Yes, but only in the truest meaning of the word—not a corner lounger with a dyed moustache leering at the women as they go by . . .

After passing the usual greetings you would take a stroll uptown as far as Thirty-fourth street—that was as high as the afternoon professional pedestrian cared to ramble—to be greeted by such beautiful and attractive women as Marie Jansen, Kate Forsythe, Pauline Hall . . . dainty Mollie Fuller . . . the Hanley sisters . . . the wonderful Lillian Russell (almost as beautiful then as she is now!) . . . Mrs. Fiske, haughty Rose Bytinge, and the regal Ada Rehan . . .

I always put up at the Union Square Hotel where, after a hurried bath and a shave, I would rush down to the street below to be welcomed by my friends . . . a slap on the back from clever Louis Harrison, and an embrace—yes, even in the open!—from his talented sister Alice; a yell of greeting from dear old Matt Snyder, many times a member of my various companies. A grunt of welcome from the stoic, Sheridan Shook, and a benign smile from Edwin Booth . . .

Often the ladies of our profession would wander downtown to meet their brothers [brother actors], and here and there you would come across

DeWolf Hopper with four of New York's leading actors in the Eighties (left to right): Richard Carle, Fred Stanley, Nat Goodwin, Walter Jones, Hopper (seated). At this time Goodwin was the best-known, with Hopper a close second.

The reigning stage beauty of the
Nineties, Lillian Russell was also
a gifted singer and actress. She
and Hopper performed together
in the Weber and Fields troupe.

a group of men and women in earnest conversation under the shady trees, comparing notes and making their arrangements for the following year.

Dainty Kate Claxton you'd find talking with A.M. Palmer on the sidewalk in front of the Union Square Theater. Maggie Mitchell, prettily tripping across the avenue from the Morton House, would smilingly acknowledge the respectful doffing of hats. The fascinating Joe Emmett would chirp merrily on his way, holding those ladies and others enthralled.

In those days no arbitrary booking organization held sway. We were all on our own, master's of our own enterprises. Like brokers on the curb we arranged our bookings on the street. Hither and thither we flew procuring a week in Pittsburgh or a night in Dayton or a two week's tour in the sunny south, or four in the unattractive middle west . . .

The day was thus occupied until three, when all work was suspended. Then we would select our own coterie of friends and adjourn to Charlie Collins Cafe, where the balance of the day was given to food, drink, anecdote, and song [and no doubt a performance to be given that night, he forgets to add].

Met less often along the Rialto, as Goodwin mentions elsewhere, would be the ravishing Lilly Langtry, in 1888 readying a nationwide tour, the exciting Richard Mansfield, the divine

*DeWolf Hopper (first left) lends an arm to his co-star
Lillian Russell. Next in line are Lew Fields, John J. Kelly,
Tom Williams, and the greatly popular Fay Templeton, all
of the Weber & Fields Company.*

The hugely popular Tony Pastor's Theater, at Union Square. Here Lillian Russell began her career.

Lower Broadway about 1888. A mile north on the left was Wallack's Theater.

Start of the mile-long stretch of Broadway known in the Eighties as The Rialto: Union Square at 16th Street.

Sarah Bernhardt, the amazingly accomplished Maurice Barrymore (father of John, Ethel, and Lionel), and that wildly popular hero of the plains, Buffalo Bill. Also, the elegant Maxine Elliott, the Polish sensation Modjeska (her first name was Helena, but nobody used it), Lotta Crabtree, bold Charlotte Cushman, and sober-faced Laura Keene (still unable to forget the night she was onstage at Ford's Theater in Washington and Lincoln was shot and she held his bloody head in her lap). Often seen were the two most famous foreign imports, Italy's dramatic sensation Tommaso Salvini (the world's greatest actor, many called him), and the premier French comic, Coquelin.

Sometimes two famous, non-theatrical names could be glimpsed: Alexander Graham Bell and Thomas Edison. If you were a New Yorker in the 1880s you talked excitedly about the wonders these two inventors had dreamed up—the telephone, of course, then not ten years old and still scarce, but particularly the stunningly unbelievable phonograph, in that year of 1888 much in the news. To see both inventions demonstrated in some hall along the avenue you'd go a couple of miles out of your way. Real voices coming from machines!

Fifty cents general admission would get you into any of a dozen or more theaters along the Rialto or in its immediate vicinity (three times that much for a really good seat up front or in the boxes, most houses having a two-dollar top). A hit was any production that held the stage for five or six weeks, say fifty performances, a minor hit, not a smash. Occasionally a show might run two or three or even four months. A six-month run or longer might come along every three or four years.

Full houses during a thirty-day run in an eight hundred-seat house could bring in $15,000, of which about a third might be clear profit. But the pool of New York theatergoers wasn't huge in the Eighties—the city's population wasn't much more than a million, at most say a million and a half. Knowing when to change the bill and mount a new show, deciding how far ahead to ready the new entry, were decisions that kept managers awake at night. Summer, winter, and fall, the competition among the city's two dozen theaters was fierce.

The rest of the story of the New York stage in 1888 can be read in the "Amusements" section from the *Times*:

5

TALLY-HO TO THE POLO GROUNDS, AUGUST 14, 1888

UDDENLY IN JULY THE GIANTS ERUPTED. TO THE INFINITE delight of the New York fans, in one great surge they won 16 of 20 games and vaulted all the way from fourth place into the lead. On the last day of the month they took sole possession of first place, then promptly reeled off another eight straight wins. By the time their principal rivals, Chicago, came to town in August, the Giants were up by six games, and the White Stockings were struggling.

Meantime, *Prince Methusalem* had opened as planned at Wallack's on July 16, to a barrage of raves, so neither Hopper nor Bell was able to join the happy throngs at the Polo Grounds for any of the three Chicago games. Though welcomed extravagantly, the show was still shaking down to the start of August, being polished and refined (prior rehearsal time hadn't been nearly enough), and its stars couldn't be spared even for an afternoon.

While the entire cast and production of *Methusalem* came in for a share of plaudits from the critics, again it was Hopper whose star shone most splendidly. When he made his grand entrance on stage as Sigismund, Prince of Trocadero, reported the *Herald*, it was to a storm of applause: "he was so heartily welcomed that he had to stand and smile his thanks for a minute or so before he began his lines with 'God bless you!'" Throughout the evening, added the *Evening Post*, the tall comedian "was uproariously funny as Sigismund," especially in his big show-stopping number: "he'd exhausted all his verses in the topical song, 'The Dotlet On the I,' long before the audience was willing to have him stop." Before the audience would let the show go on he had to repeat the number from first verse to last.

In this new work Hopper had been gifted with another great virtuoso number, even more of a smash than his big showpiece in *Tiger*, also offering a series of humorous or satiric comments on various matters of current interest in city and nation, the rollicking "Dotlet On the I." As the show went along new verses were written for the song until its length was nearly doubled. "It was a brilliant piece of writing," recalled Francis Wilson who had earlier played the Hopper role, "and helped by its lilting melody it won extraordinary popularity."

With his appearance in *Methusalem*, Hopper at last achieved the top rank in the world of operetta. Now he was only a step away from true, first-magnitude theatrical stardom (that would come in 1891 with his appearance in the smash hit *WANG*, an original American work suggested by Gilbert and Sullivan's *The Mikado*). A description of Hopper

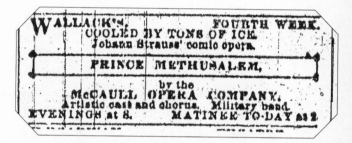

Newspaper ads for Prince Methusalem, *the comic opera in which DeWolf Hopper introduced* Casey at the Bat *to an audience. A Johann Strauss revival, it played Wallack's Theater for a month in the summer of 1888.*

in performance written later fully fits him at the moment of his *Methusalem* triumph: "his singing is so tremendously good, and his personality so overwhelming that the mightiest prejudices roll away . . . His own sense of humor is contagiously magnetic, and he certainly sings with greater force and melody, with more real art, than any of the hundred comedians who trample proftlessly upon the fragile cloud-edges of opera bouffe. . . . He is a fabulous entertainer."

It was at this moment of high triumph for both the New York theater and New York baseball that an alert fate brought the two worlds together around the magical lines and stanzas of Ernest Thayer's inspired ballad. The process was a bit roundabout and haphazard, the outcome in some doubt until almost moments before the curtain went up.

When, by month's end, the surging Giants took over sole possession of first place, Hopper and Bell were ready with a suggestion: why not recognize, at least in a small way, the fever of enthusiasm over big-league baseball that had descended on the town? A highlight of the show's last act was a raucous burlesque parade of the chorus back and forth across the stage, led by a blaring brass band. Maybe add some bit of business to this feature, nothing big, just enough to raise a cheer and get a laugh. McCaull agreed and the next night, as the *Times* noted several days later, the parade ended "with a travesty of the baseball craze, one carrying a huge bat, another an outsize ball, a third wearing a bird-cage over his head to serve as a catcher's mask, and the fourth carrying a placard with the inscription, Philadelphia, all walking dejectedly. This hit on the possibilities of the baseball season for a defeated club is received with roars of laughter nightly."

Poor Philadelphia, the target of all New York jokes, fast-fading in the pennant race, had sunk to fourth, only a game away from falling into a tie for sixth with Boston and Pittsburgh.

The idea of carrying further and expanding this humorous salute to New York's pennant fever, honoring baseball in general, also came from Hopper and Bell, with McCaull quickly agreeing. Soon after the start of August it was decided Wallack's and *Prince Methusalem* would host a "Baseball Night." The entire Giants team, along with whatever opponent was in town at the time, would be the invited guests of the house for a performance of *Methusalem*, the two teams occupying the spacious boxes flanking both sides of the hall. For Hopper's big number, "'The Dotlet On the I," new verses would be written offering humorous comment on the pennant race and predicting a championship for New York, its first. The Giants' owner, John Day, and manager Mutrie, when told, thought it a great idea, and they then issued an invitation of their own: that same day the entire cast of *Prince Methusalem* would be the guests of the Giants organization at the Polo Grounds, occupying box seats along the third-base line. The game would be over by late afternoon, say about five o'clock, leaving plenty of time for the cast to get back to the theater for the eight o'clock curtain.

A date for the event was soon chosen: Tuesday, August 14, when the visiting team would be Chicago, the Giants' principal rivals. Individually the Chicago players were popular in New York, especially Cap Anson, Fred Pfeffer, Abner Dalrymple, Pony Ryan, and Ned Williamson. The publicity release announcing the event was brief and a little tantalizing. A copy was sent to all the New York papers, most of whom ran it, whole or shortened:

SINGERS ON THE BALL FIELD

The entire McCaull Opera Company, headed by Mr. DeWolf Hopper, who is known as a baseball enthusiast, will be the guests of manager Mutrie at the Polo Grounds on Tuesday, August 14, to witness the baseball game between the New York Giants and the Chicago White Stockings. The company will start from Wallack's Theater in Tally-Ho coaches. In the evening the New York and Chicago clubs will occupy the boxes at Wallack's for a performance of *Prince Methusalem*. To properly mark the occasion, Mr. Hopper will add some baseball verses to his highly popular topical song.

At his home in a 43rd Street brownstone, on Monday August 13, Archibald Gunter picked up a newspaper, read the notice of MCaull's baseball night, then pulled out his wallet and fished in it for the *Examiner* clipping. Here, he thought, was a bit just made for a baseball celebration. Walking the half mile down to the theater, he found McCaull in his office. "I've got a little item that'd be perfect for tomorrow night's show," he told his friend, handing him the clipping. "Cut it from a Frisco paper when I was there in June. Young Hopper'd be great doing it as a recitation, I mean if there's time."

McCaull took the slip of paper; read rapidly through the poem, and as he finished laughed broadly. Yes, he agreed, it was good. With some fifty or sixty baseball people in the audience, the players and team officials with their wives, the story of Mudville's mighty slugger would fit nicely into the event—a fine addition to the new baseball verses in Hopper's big song.

He could just imagine, added McCaull with a smile, when the poem's last line sounded on the stage depicting Casey's prodigious strike-out, how the real-life sluggers in the boxes would be ruefully remembering themselves any number of times in just that role! Ewing, Anson, Connor, Tiernan, Ryan, Van Haltren—each would have his painful memories of a Casey-like ending to some crucial game. Besides being great fun, the poem might even help soften such woeful recollections!

But the piece was a lengthy one, and verbally tricky. Not so easy to memorize a script when everything depended on the subtleties of language. McCaull made a quick count: thirteen stanzas of four lines each, and a widely varied vocabulary. Hopper was the right one to do it, no question, agreed the manager, and the young actor was a fairly quick study. No doubt he'd need only a couple or three hours, maybe four, to get it by heart, decide on an approach and refine the delivery, and get in some practice. But here it was already late Monday afternoon, and with the big night scarcely twenty-four hours away. Next day there wouldn't be much time, if any, for memorizing, what with piling everyone including Hopper into the Tally-Ho coaches and up to the ball park for the Chicago-New York game, and back in time for the show.

If they were going to do the poem, then Hopper'd have to get it down pat before he went to bed that night.

"Quick!" shouted McCaull to his assistant, "get hold of Mr. Hopper. Ask him to come here to the office. Tell him we're adding a bit for tomorrow. Tell him it's a poem he'll have to commit. Tell him it's fifty-two lines . . . no, I *don't* know where he is!"

Surely the strangest fad in New York's high society in the 1880s was the so-called Tally-Ho coaching craze. Many young men whose family wealth left them with little to do and abundant time on their hands turned themselves into something like working men, with jobs to do. Joining the city's exclusive Coaching Club, they became part-time stagecoach drivers, carrying paying passengers on a regular schedule.

The stages, owned by the drivers, were all of the large, English Tally-Ho variety, able to accommodate a dozen men and women. Half sat inside in upholstered luxury, and half on comfortably padded leather cushions outside, facing fore and aft. Several times each week the coaches made long, scheduled runs from designated spots in lower New York City—the Astor House, for instance, or the Holland—to outlying parts of the Bronx or Westchester. Upon arrival at their terminus, those passengers who hadn't debarked along the way would enjoy a leisurely meal in an elegant restaurant. They would then return to the city by a different route. The idea made an immediate hit with ordinary New Yorkers, and the stages were always full, many of the seats booked well in advance.

"If you were able to pay," explains one historian, "you could enjoy the privilege of having a distinguished million-

aire like Alfred Vanderbilt serve as your coachman because
he considered this humble but expensive vocation to be a
fashionable sport."

Which of the young millionaires in the Coaching Club
may have driven the McCaull Company to the Polo Grounds
isn't recorded. Probably it can safely be guessed that every
one of the eminent idlers volunteered himself and his vehicle
for the glamorous assignment.

It was noontime on Tuesday, August 14, when pedes-
trians along Broadway looked up to see three big coaches
slowly approaching in the midst of heavy traffic along the
avenue from the south. Each was drawn by four horses, bays
or chestnuts. Each had a liveried, top-hatted driver holding
the reins. (dark-green cutaway coats with brass buttons and
a *white* topper). At the curb before Wallack's Theater, one
after another they pulled up and halted as a crowd of chattering men and women streamed from the tall, square theater
entrance.

The day was warm and bright, so those who reached
the coaches first climbed onto the high outside seats, front
and back. The stragglers had to be content with the cush-
ioned though rather cramped, rather stuffy interior.

The route uptown to the Polo Grounds lay through
Central Park, and no one was in a hurry, so the unusual pro-
cession didn't arrive at its destination until almost three
o'clock, with game time set for three-thirty. Entering through
a gate in the outfield fence, all three carriages drew up on the
outfield grass, allowing the crowd of happy riders to debark
and—to the hearty applause of the crowd—cross the infield
to their reserved seats along the third base line.

A Tally-Ho coach of New York City in the Eighties, leaving the Holland House. On the outside seats are seven passengers. Inside would sit another half-dozen. Three such coaches carried the McCaull Light Opera Company up to the Polo Grounds the afternoon of Casey's debut.

The presence of the actors at the game had helped swell the crowd to more than double its usual weekday attendance, well over 10,000, many of whom could not get into the park. "Not only the two tiers but the roof of the grandstand was packed," noted the *Herald*. "There wasn't an inch of unoccupied space on the bleaching boards. Behind the picket fences and along the rope that was stretched across the field [the far edge of the outfield, allowing room for standees] thousands were jammed together six and eight deep, while the roofs of the neighboring houses and the tops of the telegraph poles about the ground were black with people."

The first game of this three-game series between the Giants and the White Stockings, played the previous day, had been an exciting thirteen-inning draw, finally called on account of darkness. In the ninth inning, with New York behind 5-1, the Giants had scored four quick runs to tie, an explosive interlude well-described by the newspaper accounts, especially the tying run.

The action started with Connor, Richardson, and O'Rourke all hitting safely to load the bases. That brought up Ewing, who lined a single to center scoring Richardson and Connor, with O'Rourke taking third. On the next pitch Ewing broke for second, The Chicago catcher's throw was wild, allowing O'Rourke to score, while Ewing stopped at third. The next batter, Whitney, caught hold of one and sent it flying to deep center field. "While all this was going on," noted the *Herald*, "there was such a fearful racket that you couldn't hear the umpire's decisions. Cheers, hurrahs, applause, catcalls, howls, and groans filled the air, and all were united in one mighty 'Hey! Hey! Hey!' when New York tied the score."

The real drama of the sequence lay in Ewing's dash in from third on Whitney's long fly. The New York *Times*' account of it attains something of the same heightened air and elevated tone that would be heard in Hopper's recital from the stage of Wallack's Theater that evening. The score was 5 to 4, with Ewing on third and only one man out when Whitney stepped into the box while "the crowd remained silent" awaiting the first pitch:

> . . . it came shortly, and Whitney hit the ball to right field, out of Anson's reach, but sturdy little Duffy started for it and managed to capture the sphere just over the foul line where the wind had carried it. As soon as the ball settled in Duffy's hands, Ewing started for home with the speed of a sprint runner [and Duffy got off a prodigious throw to the plate].
>
> Quiet reigned on the grounds. Every eye was strained and every neck craned watching the base-runner, the fielder, and the flight of the ball as it sped on a high arc toward home.
>
> Ewing got to the plate about one foot in advance of the ball, and a joyous shout such as is seldom heard on a ball field went up from the assembled multitude.

The silent crowd "awaiting the result"—"sturdy little Duffy" galloping to the foul line in a heroic effort to "cap-

Orator O'Rourke, Giants
left-fielder, feared hitter,
and defensive ace.

Monte Ward, Giants
premier short stop.

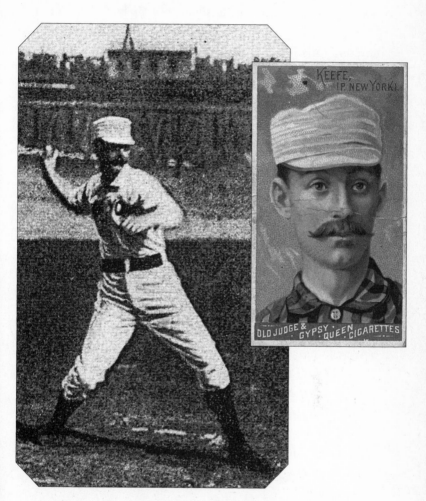

A rare action photo of the great Tim Keefe at the Polo Grounds. (Action photos of 19th century baseball are not plentiful.) It was the day of Casey's debut, and Keefe's record nineteen straight win streak was broken. Above, right, Keefe as seen on a baseball card

ture the sphere"—the "joyous shout" sent up by the "assembled multitude"—all quite standard baseball writing of the
day, and little if any different from the voice that speaks in
Casey.

The game on the August 14, played before the McCaull
Company, wasn't nearly so exciting, and to make matters
worse the Giants lost 4-2. Further, the bitter disappointment
felt by the Giant fans wasn't only because of the loss. Pitcher
Tim Keefe, the Giants ace, entered the game with a record-
breaking 19 straight wins (not equaled until Rube
Marquard's 1912 season, and never since). Everyone was
pulling for him to make it an even twenty, but his teammates
failed to hit and Keefe took the loss. For the Giants, the
game's sole highlight was a long-distance home-run blast by
Tiernan.

Not until the very last out, however, did the members
of the McCaull Company concede defeat. As the *Times*
observed, "they kept cheering the New Yorks from start to
finish. DeWolf Hopper was exasperated [by the loss], and if
comedians could weep he certainly would have done so."
The two leading ladies of the cast, Miss Cottrelly and Miss
Manola, thought it was "the height of impoliteness on the
part of Mr. Anson and his men to take a game from the
Giants when the latter were at home and in the bosom of
their families."

6

WALLACK'S THEATER, AUGUST 1888, EVENING, ENTER *CASEY*

ALL DRESSED IN DARK SUITS WITH HIGH OR WINGED COLLARS and derby hats, more than half sporting bushy moustaches, the players arrived at Wallack's Theater separately, many with their wives. They congregated in the lobby until both teams had assembled. Then they marched in together, Chicago first, to be greeted by the sprightly strains of "The Baseball Song," a hit published some weeks before (still years away was "Take Me Out to the Ball Game").

All the available seats were filled, as well as every inch of standing room. The audience—apart from the players, their wives, and team officials—numbered more than a thousand. "The house was packed to the doors," said the New York *World*, "and as the two teams came in they were given an ovation."

Wallack's was one of New York's newer theaters, having been built only six years before. Well designed, its stage was unusually high-ceilinged, and its three-tiered balcony was steeply pitched, so that every seat in the house had an excellent view. Its boxes, with elegant carvings on their golden facades, were also three-tiered. The Chicago and New York players and their guests were assigned to the first floor boxes, the first four on either side. Occupants of the two leading boxes, left and right, were no more than thirty feet or so from stage-front, center.

On the right (looking out from the stage) sat the Giants. On the left were the White Stockings. The two lead boxes held the team owners, managers, and captains—Anson for Chicago, Ewing for New York.

A few minutes before curtain time a rustle of excitement ran through the audience, and all eyes sought a tall, distinguished figure walking down the center aisle. Whispers of "General Sherman!" could be heard running through the crowd. The sixty-eight-year-old William Tecumseh Sherman, Civil War hero of the famous March to the Sea, and who had rejected a nomination for President of the United States, was another invited guest of McCaull, who knew that his friend loved both the theater and baseball. In accepting the invitation, Sherman had asked that the orchestra be told *not* to strike up *Marching Through Georgia* when he entered. By now he couldn't appear anywhere in the vicinity of a musical instrument without hearing the upbeat strains of the martial melody that had become his personal anthem (rather like "Hail to the Chief" for the president). On this night at Wallack's the orchestra stayed silent, but Sherman was recognized anyway, and some brief clapping broke out. Bowing and smiling an acknowledgment, Sherman slipped into his seat in the tenth row, center.

Wallack's Theater where DeWolf Hopper first introduced Casey at the Bat *to an audience. On Broadway at the southwest corner of 30th Street, it was New York's newest theater, often used for productions of McCaull Light Opera Company.*

A few minutes later came the overture, a lively interlude. Another few minutes, and the tall, heavy curtain parted.

The book of *Prince Methusalem* (written originally in German by Karl Truemann) was the usual light-hearted nonsense, in this case involving two mythical kingdoms, Trocadero and Riccarac, and their rulers. Hopper played Prince Sigismund, ruler of Trocadero. His daughter, Pulcinella, is betrothed to Prince Methusalem, son of Riccarac's ruler, Duke Cyprian. The two countries are about to conclude a military treaty, and the young royals are actually married. Before they can consummate the union, however, unexpected trouble arises between the two countries, so that the lovers are separated and kept apart. . . but enough of this nonsense about palace intrigue and thwarted love!

What counts in a Strauss operetta is not the silly plot, but the music, the big numbers. In this operetta the biggest number comes in Act II, Scene 2, and was sung by Hopper.

The scene opens on a room in the Trocadero palace, with two frustrated lovers, the Prince and Pulcinella, "discovered on a sofa." They sing a love duet, then hear someone approaching. Methusalem scampers off, and Pulcinella hides behind a curtain. Sigismund/Hopper, elaborately costumed, enters trailed by four pages—the difference in height between the very tall Hopper and the little page boys is extreme. Hopper strides broodingly around the stage, stops short to say something, and the pages bump into him and fall down in roly-poly fashion.

For the next ten minutes various characters enter, exchange dialogue with Sigismund, advancing and complicating, then uncomplicating, the screwball plot. All remain on stage, taking seats at a large oval table at stage center.

When finally the stage is crowded, Duke Cyprian enters, and Pulcinella reveals herself. A messenger comes in with good news—by now no one understands what he's talking about—but Sigismund/Hopper issues an invitation:

SIG: Sit down, eat, drink, and be merry. We'll have a howling spree, and no mistake.

CYP: Suppose I sing a song for you.

ALL: No! (*jumping up in protest then sitting down*)

SIG: I know a better plan than that. I've written some verses. We can make a tune for them. I call them *The Dotlet On the I.*

ALL: What's a dotlet?

SIG: A dotlet's a little dot, of course. Same as a streamlet's a little stream, or a brooklet's a little brook.

CYP: Or a hamlet's a little ham.

SIG: Yes. Or a bullet's a little bull. Here goes, then, for *The Dotlet On the I.*

(*orchestra strikes up.* SIG. *rises, dances his way around to stage-front, holds for a couple of beats, then breaks into song*)

The melody is irresistably lilting, the pace moderately fast, but what precise verses Hopper sang that night unfortunately can't be said. On the show's opening a month before, the papers reported that the big song included "a number of new verses dealing with subjects of current interest." None of them have survived. All that remains are two different sets of words from an earlier production, available now in some of the prompt books and original vocal scores. They at least give some idea of the song's style and approach.

Backing up Hopper as he sang was a chorus of all the people on stage (now including some of the actual chorus), which picks up and repeats the final four lines of each verse as he finishes it. As the chorus lustily responds, the towering Hopper does a few stylized little dance-step in place:

> Once on a time a learned man
> A letter did indite,
> But for some cause or other, none
> Could read what he did write:
>> At last it was discovered,
>> to everyone's surprise,
>> The man he did entirely
>> Forget to dot his I's!

> Through each man's life, and every day
> Our sweets seem not quite sweet
> Until a trifle comes its way
> To make a joy complete;
> A trifle 'tis to make or miss
> The very crown of bliss.
>> There is no plan or plotlet
>> Which trifles dare defy,
>> The trifle is the dotlet,
>> The dotlet on the I.

Suzette and Oscar long had wished
Their fortunes to unite,
But still they little headway made,
For both were bashful quite.
At last he dared a kiss to steal,
Which did their union seal.
        With joy their hearts did flutter,
        And it was in this wise,
        That Oscar for the first time
        Began to dot his I's!

A couple living in this town
Quite many children had;
But as they chanced to be all girls
The par-i-ents felt bad.
At last they got a bouncing boy,
Who can describe their joy!
        What they so long had wanted
        The baby boy supplies.
        They feel that now they've got it,
        The dot to crown their I's!

Chorus:
There is no plan or plotlet, etc.

After reeling off a dozen such observations on those
lucky people who finally get to dot their I's, each welcomed
by the audience with enthusiastic laughter—as much because
of the music and the insinuating artistry of Hopper and the
chorus, as for the lyrics—came what all were waiting to hear

From this ample stage in Wallack's Theater, in August 1888, Hopper first gave his dramatic recital of Casey at the Bat. *In the lower box seats on either side sat the New York and Chicago players and their guests.*

View from the stage of Wallack's Theater (about 1890), as DeWolf Hopper would have seen the audience the night he gave his first Casey performance in August 1888. The box seats occupied by the Giants and White Stockings teams are out of camera range on either side (one box can just be seen on the right margin, second level).

especially the ball players, the new baseball stanzas. Regretably none of these have survived either, but they would have offered humorous comment on the teams, the individual players, and New York's pennant chances, each verse invoking the dot-let on the I. They could not have been very hard to write. Something perhaps like these:

> For many years great Anson yearned
> To own a pennant grand,
> No other prize to him so dear,
> Yet no pennant came to hand.
> At last he found the great King Kel,
> Who hit, and ran, and played so well.
>> Then Anse four times a pennant gained
>> The secret you all have forgot!
>> It took an I-rish-man, it did,
>> Ol' Anse's I to Dot!

> Now Ewing, Tiernan, Connor, and Ward
> Bend forward on the field;
> Keefe's fastball to Van Haltren speeds:
> Will he hit or will he yield?
> If he a double can deliver
> The winning run comes over!
>> Van Haltren swings, and there it goes,
>> The spheroid sailing high, so high—
>> But a puny, pop-up fow-al
>> Crowns New York's Giant I!

> The dotlet missing from our I
> Here in New York town,

Makes cranky every true-blue crank
From Mayor Hewitt down.
Six years is much too long, you know,
Pennant-less for us to go!
   But now, my friends, I guarantee,
   And loudly do I cry,
   October next will see that flag
   Waving atop our I,
   Our I!
   The crown that dots the I!

Accompanied by thunderous applause, two ushers come down the aisle carrying, as the papers noted, a huge bunch of flowers shaped like a baseball. A band wrapped around it proclaims the "Chicago Baseball Club" as the bestower. The ushers lift it up to Hopper, who bends to receive it.

Smiling and bowing his appreciation, he waits until there is comparative quiet. "Ladies and gentlemen," he says softly, moving a little forward to the footlights. "Since we're in a baseball mood tonight, well, I have a little story about a very special moment in a very special game that I think you might like to hear. Shall I tell it?"

Applause again breaks out, with shouts from the ballplayers "Yes! Yes! Tell it!"

"It's a poem. A ballad. Goes on for five or six minutes. Still want to hear it? Or shall we get back to affairs in Trocadero?"

More applause and shouts from the boxes: "The baseball ballad! Go ahead. Let's have it!"

"It's about a team from a city called Mudville," explains Hopper. "I don't know where that is. I suppose it might be anywhere." He moves to a spot a little to stage right where the lighting has already been prepared for him. The upper half of his tall, costumed figure grows suddenly brighter.

"The outlook," he begins casually, then pauses a few seconds as if trying to recall the words. Then he comes another step forward and begins again, this time in a low tone, vibrant but relaxed, not quite matter-of-fact, but speaking fairly rapidly. His voice is strong and deep, easily carrying out over the silent listeners.*

Inconspicuous in the pit, just below Hopper, stands a prompter holding several sheets of paper under a shielded light. As Hopper later claimed, memorizing the poem had taken him "less than an hour"—which in actors' parlance means about two hours—but there'd been little time for rehearsal. With a prompter nearby he feels safer. On the prompter's sheets the poem, copied from Gunter's *Examiner* clipping, is broken up into shorter lines for easier reading. As Hopper recites, the prompter silently reads each word along with him. To every line Hopper gives added color by sustaining a tone or varying pitch, pace, and volume. With some phrases he changes his voice to suggest other speakers, including Casey himself:

---

* My comments and descriptions are based on study of Hopper's three recordings of the poem (1906, 1913, 1926, all for Victor, on 12-inch records). At times, to suit the needs of the spoken rhythm, he drops or changes a word or phrase of the original. All of these changes are included here, without special notice.

The outlook wasn't brilliant
    for the Mudville nine that day;
The score stood four to two
    With but one inning more to play;
So when Cooney died at first
    and Barrows did the same,
A sickly silence fell upon
    the patrons of the game.

A straggling few got up in
    deep despair. The rest
Clung to the hope which springs
    eternal in the human breast;
They thought if only Casey could
    but get a whack at that—
They'd put up even money now
    with Casey at the bat.

For those last two lines Hopper slowed his pace, stressed each word, and lifted his tone into a high nasal drawl, suggesting a rabid fan shouting from the stands. As he goes on, here and there he throws in an arbitrary note separating sound from sense and adding texture to the lines—a throaty whisper, a whining screech, a sonorous rumble. Repeatedly loud laughter bursts from the audience, at moments becoming, as one witness recalled, "uproarious." The next two stanzas went by fairly rapidly:

But Flynn preceded Casey,
    as did also Jimmy Blake,

And the former was a no-good,
    and the latter was a fake.
So upon that stricken multitude
    grim melancholy sat,
For there seemed but little chance
    Of Casey's getting to the bat.

But Flynn let drive a single,
    to the wonderment of all,
And Blake, the much despised,
    tore the cover off the ball;
And when the dust had lifted
    and the men saw what had occurred,
There was Jimmy safe at second,
    and Flynn a-hugging third.

Mention in the next stanza of a valley, a dell, a mountain, and a flat preserve Thayer's memory of the ball park in San Francisco, which was set in the midst of such features. Hopper gave the lines at a measured speed until he reached the word "mighty" in the last line. Framing it between two pauses, he pronounced it with a deep, gutteral emphasis, dropping a verbal curtain, so to speak, between the first and second scenes of the one-act play:

Then from five thousand throats there
    Went up a lusty yell;
It rumbled through the valley,
    it rattled in the dell;
It knocked upon the mountain-top,
    and recoiled upon the flat,

> For Casey, mighty Casey, was
>   advancing to the bat.

Casey's proud, smiling presence as he steps into the batter's box and takes his stance is well sketched in the next stanza, as is his pausing for his usual lordly gesture of acknowledgement to the cheering crowd. In the stanza's final line, as Hopper always delivered it, the high-pitched, suddenly satirical note strongly suggests an excited female fan in the stands swooning loudly over the glamorous batsman:

> There was pride in Casey's bearing
>   As he stepped into his place,
> There was ease in Casey's manner,
>   and a smile on Casey's face.
> And when, responding to the cheers,
>   he lightly doffed his hat,
> No stranger in the crowd could doubt
>   'twas Casey at the bat.
>
> Ten thousand eyes were on him.
>   as he rubbed his hands with dirt;
> Ten thousand hands applauded
>   When he wiped them on his shirt.
> Then while the writhing pitcher
>   ground the ball into his hip,
> Defiance gleamed in Casey's eye,
>   a sneer curled Casey's lip.

The term "writhing" is a neatly teasing way of describing a pitcher going into an elaborate wind-up. But why does he grind the ball "into his hip"? That was a borrowing from cricket, whose bowlers did the same, and for the same reason, to scuff up or roughen a portion of the ball's surface, helping it to curve. The practice was long since dropped in baseball, but continues in cricket.

That marvelously superior "sneer" in the last line was given particular prominence by Hopper, a final characterization of the "mighty" batsman, further setting him up for his awful fate.

> And now the leather-covered sphere
>   came hurtling through the air,
> And Casey stood a-watching it
>   in lofty grandeur there;
> Close by the sturdy batsman
>   the ball unheeded sped—
> "That ain't my style," said Casey.
>   "Strike one," the umpire said.

The umpire's "strike one" comes suddenly out of Hopper's mouth in a high, piercing tone, almost a screech— *stee-rike one!*—strongly suggesting the call of an actual umpire, and gently satirizing those more histrionically inclined (there were a few even then). The same type of emphasis he used to deliver the time-honored phrase in line five of the next stanza:

> From the benches, black with people,
>   there went up a muffled roar,
> Like the beating of the storm-waves
>   on a stern and distant shore.

"Kill him! Kill the umpire!"
        shouted someone in the stand;
And it's likely they'd have killed him
        had not Casey raised his hand.

With a smile of Christian charity
        great Casey's visage shone;
He stilled the rising tumult,
        he bade the game go on;
He signaled to the pitcher, and
        once more the spheroid flew;
But Casey still ignored it, and
        the umpire said "strike two."

Again, when delivering the dread words "strike two,"
Hopper used that same sustained screech, letting his voice
trail off as if it were an echo.

For every line in the next stanza Hopper pulled out all the
stops, his powerful, vibrant voice signaling that the climax had
been reached. In lines three and four with each syllable he
drops his voice until the final word becomes a drawn-out rumble ("B flat below low C," he identified the note). It provided
another curtain, also drawing much laughter, and giving the
audience a momentary rest before the rapid denouement. From
here to the poem's close his mellow voice takes on an extra
shading, many words being intoned, almost sung.

"Fraud!" cried the maddened thousands,
        and echo answered fraud;
But one scornful look from Casey
        and the audience was awed.

They saw his face grow stern and cold,
　　They saw his muscles strain,
And they knew that Casey wouldn't
　　let that ball go by again.

The sneer is gone from Casey's lip,
　　his teeth are clenched in hate,
He pounds with cruel violence
　　his bat upon the plate.
And now the pitcher holds the ball,
　　and now he lets it go,
And now the air is shattered by
　　the force of Casey's blow.

A pause . . . in the hushed hall the unusual word *shattered* shimmers and echoes. Unmoving, for a moment Hopper stares out over the audience, then slowly shifts his position, taking a couple of steps to his left, the spotlight following. When he intones the final stanza he gives its opening line a wonderfully pathetic touch, the initial "Oh" coming out as a reluctant sob:

Oh, somewhere in this favored land
　　the sun is shining bright . . .

Another slight pause, then he goes on, his tone now mournful and laden with regret:

Somewhere bands are playing,
　　and somewhere hearts are light;
Somewhere men are laughing,
　　and somewhere children shout . . .

For the final two lines of the poem Hopper ingeniously switches the emphasis. The last line he does not belabor hut gives as a plain if forlorn statement of fact. It is the next-to-last line that he highlights, pronouncing it as a slow, strangled, despairing cry from the heart:

> But there is no joy in Mudville—
> Mighty Casey has struck out.

Forlornly through the silent hall echoes the word "out." Hopper's head bows—his chin drops to his chest—his shoulders slump—his arms hang limply at his sides. Suddenly, there bursts from the audience a wave of enthusiastic applause. Over the stage it washes, along with laughter, whistling and cheers, engulfing Hopper's tall, spotlighted figure

Reporters from most of the city's larger newspapers were on hand. The recounting in three of them of the night's festivities, and of the audience reaction to Hopper's recital, leaves no doubt that the poem and Hopper's broad interpretation proved a smash hit. "The first act of *Prince Methusalem* went with its usual snap and effect," said the *Times*. "In the second act, however, were some new and pat features. DeWolf Hopper, after singing 'The Dotlet On the I,' with all the customary verses, topped them off with ones about the pennant that brought out long continued applause and laughter. In response to the demonstrations he then proceeded to recite a thrilling ode entitled 'Casey's at the Bat,' which was most uproariously received, particularly the ending, which told in mock-heroic strain how the redoubtable Casey 'struck out'. . . . Altogether it was a great evening for the nines, the company, and Col. McCaull, as well as for the large audience."

The *World* reporter has the players reacting to the recital of *Casey* a lot more demonstratively than the *Times*, and also reports some asides by Hopper: "As might be expected, Hopper let himself loose on the subject of baseball, and the players laughed heartily at the hits the comedian threw at them. . . . When he sang 'The Dotlet On the I' the house roared from beginning to end. One of the verses was about the victory of the Giants, and before he sang it he turned to the Chicagos and said, 'You have had the pennant long enough to stand this.'" When he gave *Casey*, "men got up on their seats and cheered, while old Gen. Sherman laughed until the tears ran down his cheeks. It was one of the wildest scenes ever seen in a theater and showed the popularity of Hopper and of baseball."

The *Tribune* said that Hopper's rendition of *Casey* "convulsed the audience with laughter," and it recounts a Hopper ad-lib which brought down the house:

> . . . Hopper played the leading part in a strictly baseball version of Prince Methusalem at Wallack's Theater last night . . . he was in fine form and fairly reveled in funny little baseball nothings. . . . The theater was crowded and the sign dear to theater managers, "Standing Room Only," was displayed in Broadway early in the evening . . .
>
> Hopper's song, "The Dotlet On the I," was hugely enjoyed, especially by the baseball men. Frequenters of the Polo Grounds were greatly

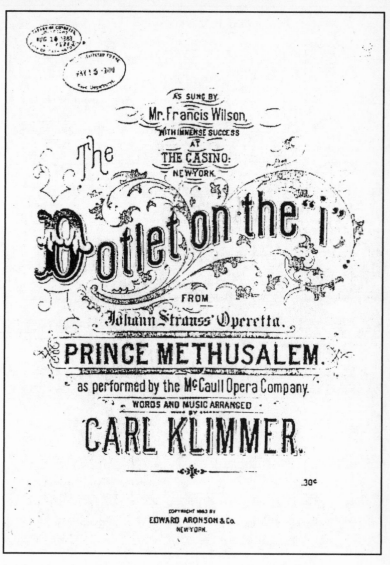

Hopper's big number in Prince Methusalem, *"The Dotlet On the I,"
which served to introduce his recital of* Casey, *when first produced
in 1883, became a popular favorite. This sheet music cover names
Hopper's predecessor in the role, his friend Francis Wilson.*

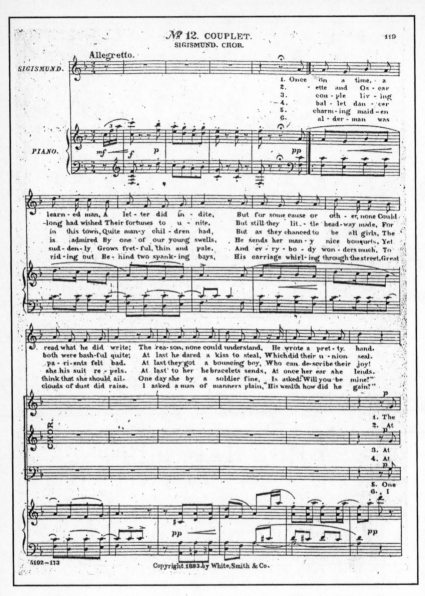

Vocal score for Hopper's big number in Prince Methusalem, *"The Dotlet On the I." To the regular lyrics he added several stanzas about baseball, and followed the song with his first recital of* Casey.

pleased when the Duke of Trocadero [Hopper] was bewailing the revolution in the kingdom to hear him scream, "Oh I can stand anything if Lynch don't umpire!"

A tremendous floral ball, a present from the Chicago club, was presented to Hopper at the close of his *Dotlet* song . . .

Thomas Lynch was one of the half-dozen umpires who worked the games at the Polo Grounds during 1888, and was least liked by the New York players, who were sure that he favored their opponents. He had worked the game on August 13, and had been loudly condemned for his calling of balls and strikes—"very severe against New York," complained the *Times*. Lynch also worked the game the next day, the day of Hopper's recitation, prompting the New York *Tribune* to rant that "Mr. Lynch's umpiring was positively nauseating."

The next day at the Polo Grounds, August 15, Lynch was back behind the plate, bringing still more charges of bias. Lynch gave a Chicago man a base on balls, shouted the *Times*, "when it was evident to nearly every person on the grounds that Welch had pitched three balls directly over the plate." In this part of the game, at least, things have been the same from the start until now.

When the clapping, and cheering, and hoorahing that followed Hopper's recitation of *Casey* had finally faded away, everyone's mood was readjusted to that other world of make-believe, a Strauss operetta, enjoying the third and final act of *Methusalem*. In the show's final minutes came the comic parade, and again baseball was invoked. Attired in

Giants uniforms, the chorus marched in behind a loud brass band, following a huge pennant held loft on a staff, bearing the words *New York*. It was well after eleven when the final curtain fell. For several minutes the hall resounded with thunders of applause as Hopper and the other principles took repeated curtain-calls.

One last twist in the story of that wonderful night at Wallack's must be put on record. It took place the very next day at the Polo Grounds, and was witnessed by Hopper, Bell, and other members of the *Methusalem* cast. No more fitting wind-up can be imagined for the whole episode, for almost the very tale of woe told by Hopper on the stage the previous night came alive on the field for seven thousand fans, a bit more than the number mentioned in the poem. In the Giants' third and last game against Chicago, the mighty—but in this case, luckless—Roger Connor wonderfully, if unwittingly, got in real life a taste of what happened to Casey in the fictional saga.

The moment came, fittingly, in the ninth inning, and with New York still two runs behind, further resembling the poem. It began with several Giants hits and—just as in the poem with the no-good Flynn and Blake the fake—when the dust had lifted and all saw what had occurred, there was Ewing safe at second and Welch a-huggin' third.

Then from seven thousand throats arose a lusty yell. It rumbled along 110th Street, and rattled in the Sixth Avenue dell. It resounded through Central Park and recoiled upon the Fifth Avenue flat. For Connor, mighty Connor, was advancing to the bat:

. . . as he walked up to the plate the audience cheered him heartily. It all depended on Connor, and he knew it. So he waited for a good ball, and finally it came, and he smashed it. Away it shot over Baldwin's head, and the people began to cheer wildly. But they suddenly stopped. For in deep center field Ryan thrust up his hands and the ball stuck to them [hands, not a glove]. So New York was whipped in a great fight.

The *World*'s closing comment on that thrilling out is more in the proper *Casey* mode. After Ryan hauled in Connor's mighty blast, "the lamentations that arose from the bleacheries were like unto those of the lost children of Israel."

A final small note rounds out the tale of *Casey*'s debut. In the New York *Herald*'s account of that last game there is a phrase that nicely echoes a line from the poem, no doubt reflecting the reporter's delight in what he heard the night before at Wallack's. The poem speaks of "the hope that springs eternal in the human breast." In the *Herald*, when the Giants bunched several hits, "hope filled every breast."

From newspaper accounts of many regular-season games, Thayer had cleverly drawn much of *Casey*'s colorful phrasing. Here a newspaper borrows from him, marking the first small acknowledgment of the celebrated poem's now unbreakable tie to the game.

7

STAR THEATER, OCTOBER 1888, ENCORE *CASEY*

THREE WEEKS AFTER CASEY'S DEBUT AT WALLACK'S, ANOTHER baseball game took place at the Polo Grounds. It had nothing to do with home runs and pitcher's duels. It was a benefit game played for an ailing actor, and starred a team of performers, led by DeWolf Hopper and Digby Bell, against a team of New York newspaper reporters. It was "one of the funniest games of baseball in sports history," thought the *Times*.

To mild cheering by the crowd of two thousand the journalists took the field, decently attired in spare Giants uniforms. Then the actors came out and "the shouts of laughter that went up as they reached the diamond must have been heard in Westchester County."

Leading the actors onto the field were Hopper and James Powers (then starring at the Casino in the smash hit comic opera *Nadjy*). Powers was clad from head to toe in "one of Marie Jansen's cast-off ballet rigs," and was prancing about with Hopper, "whose long frame was attired in a loud, striped bathing suit, a life preserver, and a straw bonnet. The sight would have made a pessimist believe there was something in life worth laughing about."

Pitching for the actors was Digby Bell, who did so not in the approved fashion but "in the best English cricket bowler style." At bat Bell hit a grounder, and when he was thrown out at first "he stood there and blubbered like a kid." Harry Clark, who was starring in *The Queen's Mate*, a big hit, with Lillian Russell—who cheered enthusiastically from the stands, attracting attention from all the males in her vicinity—did the catching for the actors clad in Giants uniforms three sizes too large. Francis Wilson, starring in the comic opera *Erminie* (Broadway's biggest hit for many a year) "looked like a stick of peppermint candy in a red-and-white striped uniform." Umpiring was the day's most famous and best-loved clown, Peter Dailey, who wore only a "a huge pair of pants with the waist up at his neck, and with his arms sticking out through the pockets."

Just before the game's start, Nick Engel, owner of a restaurant favored by the actors, led in a donkey that had a large keg of beer slung on its back. The keg was placed on a stand at third base, and any player who could get that far "was entitled to a glass of the foaming beverage."

Play during the game was on the unorthodox side: "The journalists led off with eight runs in their half of the first inning, and whitewashed the actors in their half. The actors got square in the next inning by letting three men get on base and then, after the batter hit a terrific sky-scraper to

Francis Wilson in left field, had each baseman trip the runner at his base and sit on him until Wilson came in and tagged each one with the ball, making the greatest triple play on record."

One of the biggest laughs came when Richard Goldin, a favorite comedian of the day, dressed as Herman the Magician and playing shortstop, "caught a fly ball, changed it into an egg, and threw it to the pitcher." In the eighth inning Hopper got into a furious argument with Dailey over running the wrong way on the bases, "and Dailey shot him dead with a pistol and he was carried bodily from the field."

Only once on their march to the 1888 pennant did the New Yorks stumble, causing their devoted fans to tremble. That happened a week after the big Wallack's night, when they lost four straight to Boston and King Kelly, the first four games in a six-game series. "WHAT CAN THE MATTER BE?" worried a screamer headline in the New York *World*. But the slide was halted when Ewing and company roared back to take the fifth and sixth games. After those triumphs they never looked behind them, and on October 4—fittingly, against Chicago at the Polo Grounds, before "a vast throng" including Hopper and Bell—clinched the championship.

With that Hopper and Bell again went into action, arranging another theatrical baseball night, planned to center on a formal presentation of the pennant to the Giants. Coralling their colleagues up and down Braodway, they also invited the public and charged admission, the proceeds to be

The New York Actors baseball team ready for a charity game at the old Polo Grounds in 1889. Standing at center rear is DeWolf Hopper. Seated directly in front of him is Francis Wilson (forty-seven years later Wilson will be a pall-bearer at

Hopper's funeral). This same team, mostly Broadway stars, the year before took part in "one of the funniest baseball games ever played." (for a description see text, 000-000).

shared out among the players (about $300 went to each man, a tidy sum then, about a third of the average annual baseball salary). Set for the night of October 14, it was booked into the Star Theater on lower Broadway.

With every turn done by a top Broadway Star, a round dozen of them, the stage show lasted more than two hours. Dockstader's minstrels opened the program, and DeWolf Hopper closed it. Standing alone on the stage after giving his two hit numbers, he stepped to the footlights. "What say you?" he asked. "Shall we invite our old friend the mighty Casey to be a part of our celebration?"

"Yes! yes!" screamed the crowd. "Give us Casey! Let's hear it! Casey!"

In his best casual manner, without further comment Hopper began, "The outlook wasn't brilliant," and for the second time the story of the Mudville hero came vibrantly alive on a public stage. Some six minutes later there sounded those mournful words, "mighty Casey has struck out," and the audience erupted in a salvo of wild applause. The *Times* reporter in describing the evening's festivities couldn't recall the poem's title so he made a guess: "How Casey Lost the Game."

With all the Giants on stage, presentation of the pennant followed, a large blue silk banner, framed in gold and bearing the words, "Champions 1888, N.Y.B.B.C."

In 1888 the World Series had not yet been standardized. The pennant winners of the National League, the Giants, and the American Association, the St. Louis Browns, decided matters for themselves, whether there would *be* a series, how many games, and where they'd he played. This year a ten-game series was agreed on, six wins deciding. Of the first five games, played at the Polo Grounds and Brooklyn, New York won four. The sixth game was played at Philadelphia where Hopper was heading the road cast of *The Lady or the Tiger?* In a ceremony before the game, played on October 22, Hopper and Bell were honored by the Giants, each being presented with a gold-headed walking cane inscribed, "Compliments of the N.Y.B.B. Club."

In the game itself the Giants at first fell behind and it was Roger Connor who brought them even, not with his bat but with his blazing speed on the basepaths, so unexpected in a man of his large size (in the sixth he walked, stole second, and on Ward's single came flying round third to beat the throw at the plate by a fraction). With that, Hopper and Bell received their final news coverage of the 1888 season as baseball cranks. "When Connor crossed the plate," said the New York *World*, "scoring the tieing run, wild shouts of joy went up from the admirers of the Gaints . . . the noisiest men in the party were DeWolf Hopper and Digby Bell of the McCaull Company."

The Giants' sixth and deciding win came on October 25 at St. Louis. The championship was no "trifle," as Hopper's song declared, yet New York's "I" had at last been well and truly dotted. The city's state of joyous euphoria, as it was to prove, lasted through the following year, when the Giants again took the pennant, beating Boston by a single game. In the 1889 World Series, against the Brooklyn Bridegrooms, they won again, putting in place still another dotlet.

In honor of this second straight championship, at another festive occasion featuring another parade of Broadway stars, Hopper again recited *Casey*—or say that he *performed* it. That was the last time for three years he would give the poem in public. When he did resume, it wasn't in connection with baseball (not for another fifteen years would the Giants again cop the pennant). It came as an extra added attraction in Hopper's first huge stage triumph, the show that finally catapulted him to the top.

During the three years that Hopper neglected Casey, the poem wasn't quite forgotten. None other than the King himself kept it alive.

Handsome, personable Michael J. Kelly, besides being baseball's first celebrity-superstar, was also one of the first professional athletes whose fame carried him onto the legitimate stage, certainly he was the first to do it in a serious way (boxing champions John L. Sullivan and Jim Corbett also appeared on stage at this time but mostly to be stared at). In the late Eighties Kelly had been offered parts in stage plays, and he'd actually appeared in a few in minor roles, so that he thought quite seriously about having a full-fledged acting career when his playing days were done. As his first move in that direction he took to reciting *Casey* on the music hall and variety circuit.

Only it was *Kelly at the Bat*, the name altered wherever it occurred in the poem's fifty-two lines, with mythical Mudville becoming the very real Boston. What made it acceptable for him to sing his own praises as the mighty slugger, of course, was the fact that he ends by confessing to total failure: "The mighty Kelly has struck out." In rival cities like

New York, Philadelphia, and Washington, for all the base-ball cranks that last line must have brought down the house.

Kelly was not present at any of the three Hopper performances of *Casey*, so how and where he first encountered the poem can only be guessed. Certainly he would have heard about it from the Giants players or by reading newspaper accounts of the big night at Wallack's. It is also possible that he saw the poem in print, a part of it anyway, even before Hopper did. On July 28, 1888, seven weeks after its original publication in the San Francisco *Examiner*, but two-plus weeks before that Wallack's night, eight stanzas of the poem, the final eight, were reprinted by the New York *Sporting Times*. Meant as a jibe at Kelly, his name was substituted for that of Casey throughout.

At that very time, as it happened, the Giants were in Boston for a three-game series, and no doubt the King was gleefully shown the poem by his New York opponents—the great Kelly strikes out! Ewing or O'Rourke or the wily Ward would surely have made certain that their nemesis saw a composition depicting him—by name!—as a bust at the plate. Very probably, the affable Kelly joined in the laughter against himself.

Kelly's style in reciting the poem, whether an imitation of Hopper's broad exaggeration or something quieter, is a matter lost to time. Unless a paragraph of description lurks in the yellowed pages of some old newspaper, no one who heard him left any comment, and he never recorded the poem (a curious omission). If he'd lived longer, more would be known about his direct if brief role in the rise and spread of *Casey*. Just after his baseball career drew to a close—six-

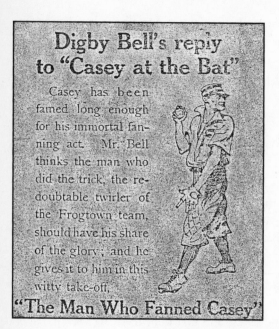

Digby Bell's reply to "Casey at the Bat"

Casey has been famed long enough for his immortal fanning act. Mr. Bell thinks the man who did the trick, the redoubtable twirler of the Frogtown team, should have his share of the glory; and he gives it to him in this witty take-off,

"The Man Who Fanned Casey"

So-called "replies" to Casey *are many. This one—* "The Man Who Fanned Casey"*—recorded by Hopper's theatrical colleague and baseball chum, Digby Bell, suggests that Casey whiffed on a spitball, in 1888 still legal.*

The Star Theater, 13th Street and Broadway, site of the 1888 National League pennant presentation to the Giants. Among the entertainment was DeWolf Hopper's second public recitation of Casey.

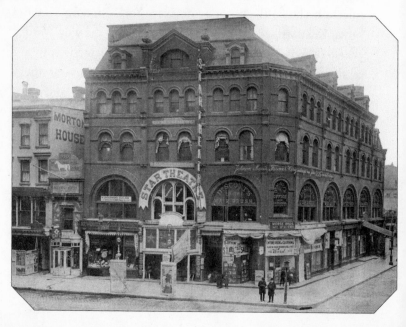

King Kelly of Boston. As Thayer was writing Casey, *in May 1888, he probably read in the papers of the heroics of Kelly against the New York Giants in a four-game series at the Polo Grounds. When Kelly began reciting* Casey *on the stage, he changed the name to* Kelly at the Bat.

teen furious years, with the end to some extent hastened by his drinking and his careless habits—he died of pneumonia in a Boston hospital. The date was December 1894. He was thirty-six years old.

In the obituaries, Kelly's fellow ballplayers, while lauding his great athletic talents, spoke of him equally in terms of friendship and their admiration of him as a man. "He was a whole-souled, genial fellow with a host of friends," said the mourning Anson, "a born humorist and an agreeable companion." His teammate Fred Pfeffer recalled him as "a jester of rich and unrivalled humor . . . a kindly, pleasant fellow." Jim Hart, who managed Boston while Kelly played there, saw him as "beyond doubt the most original character of all," and the Boston *Globe* needed a Shakespearean quote to express its admiration: "Take him for all in all, we shall not see his like again."

Simplest and best, perhaps, was the comment of the Chicago *Tribune*: "Kelly will hardly ever be forgotten while baseball is played in America."

All too soon forgotten, however, was the unique role played in the *Casey* saga by the King, first inspiring it, and then keeping it alive on the stage.

Faring much better than the King in his latter days was *Casey*'s second model, the mighty Roger Connor. Voted New York's "Most Popular Player," he retired in 1897, settling with his family in his old hometown, Waterbury, Connecticut. As owner of the minor league Waterbury team he played for seven years as its first baseman (hitting a respectable .307). Afterward, he became Inspector of Schools for Waterbury, and died there in 1931, aged seventy-five.

His passing stirred a leading sportswriter, John Kieran of the New York *Times*, to record a conversation he overheard between two old-time fans:

> . . . too bad about Roger Connor. Now there was a batter! Could he hit! . . .
>
> I always liked Roger. He was a fine player and had what you might call dignity. Lots of those fellows on the '88 team were that way—There was Orator O'Rourke, and John Ward . . . Roger was one of the first players to wear eyeglasses. He did it in his later years when his eyes got bad.
>
> A big, tall, broth of a boy was Roger . . . remember the time he hit a ball over the right-field wall at the old Polo Grounds at 110th street?
>
> I do. It was the first time anyone had ever done such a thing. An excited fan jumped up and started a collection for Roger. I'll tell you who chipped in. There was Col. McAlpin, and Senator Grady, and the Johnson whose brother was later mayor of Cleveland, the 3-cent fare man, and lots of others. They gave Roger a big gold watch, and he still had it when I saw him in Waterbury a few years ago . . .
>
> When you're talking about great players and fine men don't forget Roger Connor!

8

THE WORCESTER THEATER, 1892, ENTER HOPPER, ENTER THAYER

O NE-WORD, SINGLE SYLLABLE TITLES FOR PLAYS ARE NOT favored by theatrical producers and librettists, especially for musicals. There isn't enough to evoke dreams or to stick in the mind. The title of the operetta that in 1891 put Hopper's star over the top—*WANG*—apparently was different. When New Yorkers began flocking to see it, that explosive, one-syllable word took on a unique flavor all its own.

Opening at the Broadway Theater on May 4, with Hopper in the lead as the Regent of Siam, the new musical scored the year's biggest hit, earning nothing but raves. *WANG*, said the New York *Times*, "has achieved monumental fame at a single bound . . . the burlesque was mounted extravagantly, and the chorus sang with an abundant energy. The audience applauded everything, and demanded most of the songs a second time." Five of the songs were sung by Hopper, his big number coming with the clever and tuneful, "Ask the Man in the Moon."

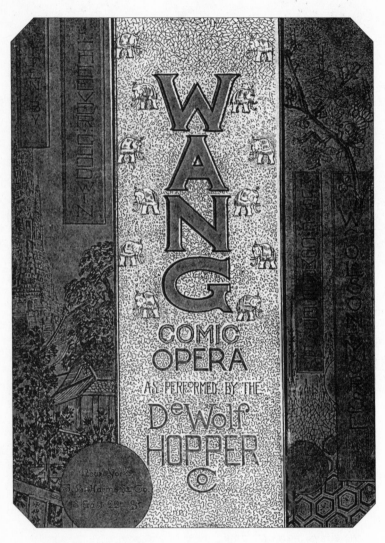

The comic opera WANG elevated DeWolf Hopper to theatrical heights, and for nearly three decades he reigned as Broadway's top star in comic opera.

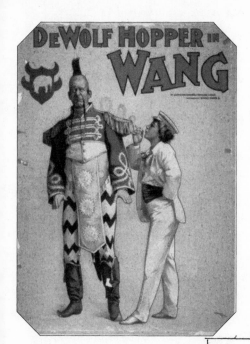

Hopper in costume for WANG *as the Regent of Siam.*

In December 1892, when WANG *played Thayer's home town of Worcester, Mass., Hopper finally met Casey's author. This ad from the Worcester* Spy *states that the cast of* WANG *numbered no fewer than 75 players, but forgot to mention the huge prop elephant.*

AMUSEMENTS, ETC.

WORCESTER THEaTRE.

ROCK & BROOKS, Proprietors and Managers.

TWO NIGHTS. | **Tues.** and **Wed., Dec. 20, 21,**

DeWOLF

HOPPER !

Presenting the jolliest of all Comic Operas,

WANG,

Set in a Frame of Gold.

With the entire ORIGINAL COMPANY of seventy-five people, direct from the Broadway Theatre, New York.

Prices: Orchestra and Orchestra Circle, $1.50; Balcony, $1; Family Circle, 7[?]c.; Admission, $1; Gallery, 25c.

Sale of seats now progressing.

Fri.-Sat., Dec. 23-24, Saturday Matinee.
Chas Frohman's Boston Stock Company direct from the Columbia Theatre, Boston, in the great success, "SURRENDER."
Usual Prices: $1, 75, 50, 25c. Sale opens Tuesday.

In *WANG*, seconded the *Post*, "DeWolf Hopper has made the hit of his career . . . packing the Broadway Theater to overflowing at every performance." The graduating class at West Point, added the paper, for its annual New York holiday had voted to attend *WANG* in a body.

More important than all the praise and the huge financial success—at least for our present subject!—it was *WANG* that revived Hopper's dormant interest in *Casey*. It was *WANG* that really started him on his life-long career as the poem's principal advocate and expounder. By now he was no longer with the McCaull group, having gone out on his own in 1890, after the close of the previous season. Digby Bell, too, had left McCaull, and that same year had found a starring vehicle of his own, the long-running *The Tar and the Tartar*. It is pleasant to think that throughout the Nineties and well into the new century the two baseball chums, while never again appearing on the same stage, reigned as Broadway's leading comic opera stars.

After running on Broadway for six months, *WANG* was getting set to go on tour. By now, as he said, Hopper felt that the show "needed an added fillip," something to perk himself up, as well as intrigue the audiences in smaller towns and cities—he was also feeling the strains always resulting from a very long theatrical run of more than one hundred fifty performances. (His longest previous run had been about half of that total.) What made him think that a baseball poem inserted into an oriental comedy would play well for a general audience he never said. The plot of *WANG*, however, was even looser and if possible sillier than *Methusalem*, so there were probably several spots to accommodate a strange, new note.

"I never thought," recalled Hopper, "of using *Casey at the Bat* regularly in the theater until the second season of *WANG*. . . . I tried it on an audience, found it what vaudeville players now call a 'wow,' and began to interpolate it nightly."

Since he'd be making regular commercial use of the piece, he felt that he needed the author's permission, and was very willing to pay any fees involved. For the first time seriously he began to wonder who the author was—before this, reciting the poem infrequently and informally, while feeling curious, the question of the identity of "Phin," the name signed to the *Examiner* printing of the poem, never seemed pressing. Now he made inquiries, expecting no difficulty, but without success. Finally he wrote directly to the *Examiner*, which proved slow to respond. He still hadn't gotten a reply from San Francisco when *WANG*'s New England tour reached Worcester, where it would play two nights, the first set for December 20, 1892.

On the December 19 a note arrived at Hopper's hotel. It was from an old friend of the Hopper family, a music teacher named Benjamin Hammond who had retired to Worcester. Would Hopper, asked the note, like to meet the author of *Casey*?

Entering the ornate front door of the exclusive Worcester Club, Hopper and Hammond checked their overcoats, then inquired for Mr. Ernest Thayer. They were ushered into one of the private rooms where leather armchairs clustered round a large fireplace in which crackled a small fire. Rising to meet them was a short, slightly-built, pleasant-faced, dark-suited man. Next to Hopper's tall bulk he looked almost like a schoolboy.

As Hammond introduced them, the two shook hands, Hopper saying what an honor and pleasure it was to meet *Casey's* creator. Thayer responded with a compliment of his own for the famous actor. Still unmarried, no longer writing, Thayer was now living a life of leisure, with frequent trips to Europe, in particular Florence, a city he loved and from which he'd recently returned.

For several hours the two talked over the poem, its background and inspiration, and discussed Thayer's brief career in journalism. Neither man made a record of the conversation, yet the disappointing omission seems not beyond recovery. Given their backgrounds, personal interests, and leanings, what might two such men at such a moment have talked about?

"I've heard wonderful things about your rendition of my poem," Thayer no doubt at one point offered. "As well as making it great fun you bring it remarkably alive, I've been told."

"Yes, people do seem to enjoy it," replied Hopper. "But the magic is mostly in the lines themselves. You yourself are the magician, Mr. Thayer. The poem is really a marvelous bit of word-sketching. It has color, action, character, a strong story-line, masterful versifying. Is it based on an actual game or incident? Some known personality?"

"No, not on any single game or incident. It's a common situation in baseball, you know. A team is trailing in the score and with men on base the leading slugger comes to bat. Do you follow baseball, Mr. Hopper? Are you a *crank?*"

"The worst kind! I get carried away sometimes, make an ungodly amount of noise! Oh, but it's a great game, isn't it? What about a model for Casey? Did you have someone in mind? Let me guess! Shall I take a guess?"

"Go ahead," laughed Thayer, "who do you think it was?"

"You *must* have had a model in mind to achieve so accurate a portrait, even if you carry it over into burlesque. Let's see. Living up here you must be a Boston fan. King Kelly, of course."

"A good man. But try again."

"Not Kelly? There's a surprise. Well, New York isn't far from Worcester. Who could it be but our staunch Roger Connor. If it's not the King then it's got to be the mighty Roger."

"Try again."

"Not Connor? Not the formidable Roger? In that case it's got to be the Detroit man, Dan Brouthers. He'd be perfect in the role, perfect! It's the great Brouthers, isn't it?"

"Keep going."

"Not Brouthers either! Well, well . . . I'd have bet a bundle it was one of the three . . . I know! Tip O'Neil."

"Tip's a good man too, but no."

"Cap Anson. It *must* be Anson."

"Not Anson."

"One of the old-timers from the Seventies. Ross Barnes."

"Not Barnes."

"Not O'Neil, Anson, or Barnes. Then *who* can . . ."

"Not one man. *All* of them. Casey is really a composite of your first three choices, mostly, with the others in the background. As I wrote I thought about one or another of them, especially the way each man carried himself, his physical presence at the plate. There was that natural swagger of the brawny Brouthers, and that tremendous swing—they don't call him Big Dan for nothing. Then Connor has that easy, graceful, rolling walk as he comes so confidently up to the plate and the way he stands there with his bat cocked, *filling* the batter's box."

"And Kelly? He's not a big man . . ."

"True, he's not. Under six feet by a couple of inches. Yet in some ways he's the biggest of them all."

"Biggest? You don't mean biggest."

"Indeed I do. When I wrote the poem back in '88 I'd seen Kelly play only once, out on the coast in a game against a Frisco team. He came up in a situation much like that of Casey, and he struck out. He's not big but . . . it's hard to describe him. A wonderfully self-possessed *air*, I guess you'd say. He *knows* what he can do, what he *might* do, *shows* that he knows it, and knows that the *other* side knows it too! In the stands the crowd may be howling hysterically but at the plate stands Kelly cool and smiling . . . his reputation makes the difference. It *enlarges* him . . ."

"Kelly, Connor, and Brouthers. You had them in mind as you wrote the poem, thought about them at the plate and hitting and so on?"

"Not constantly. Now and then, at different times. a sort of montage, I guess you could say. Mostly I pictured them swinging mightily at the ball and missing, striking out. That helped me to get just the right note of . . . parody . . . affectionate mockery."

"The poem, I remember, was published in June '88. When did you write it."

"About a month before it appeared."

"How did it end up in the *Examiner*, that little paper way out in Frisco?"

Thayer explained how he'd been a regular staffer on the *Examiner* for a year and a half, and how he'd come home and written the poem right there in Worcester, and mailed it back to the coast.

"Thank God for Archie Gunter!" blurted Hopper, and he went on to tell Thayer of the novelist's part in bringing the poem back east in time for Wallack's baseball night. "Quite a rounda-bout trip before it got to me!" laughed Hopper. "Six thousand miles to cover a distance of less than two hundred! Fate, that's what it was, fate. It was meant to be!"

"You do it in *WANG*, I understand," inquired Thayer. "Is it a regular part of the show?"

"It is for now. I use it as a sort of encore, an off-beat encore. Makes a big hit. I'm thinking I'll work it into much of what I do in the future . . . oh, but I'll need your permission of course. That's what I meant to ask about."

Before the two parted that night, Thayer gave his permission for Hopper to use the poem on stage without restriction, nor would he accept any payment. Hopper in turn extended an invitation to the poet to be his guest next night for *WANG*'s first Worcester performance.

Very curious to hear for himself how Hopper infused his ballad with life, especially in a theater before a large audience, not all of whom understood or cared for baseball, the flattered poet gratefully accepted.

By now a reporter for the city's leading newspaper, *The Spy*, had gotten wind of the meeting between author and

actor, and of the invitation to a performance. The following
evening he was on hand at the Worcester Theater, and his
account of the evening appeared in *The Spy* the next day:

> . . . a noticeable incident of the evening's perform-
> ance was Mr. Hopper's life-like recitation of "Casey
> At the Bat." As he explained to the audience, Mr.
> Hopper did not know until his present arrival in
> Worcester who was the writer of this clever, humor-
> ous poem, than which he had never found anything
> more useful for his purpose on the stage.
>
> The mention of Mr. Thayer's name was fol-
> lowed by applause, which became very enthusias-
> tic at the close of the actor's spirited and laughable
> rendition of the skit in question. Mr. Hopper
> gratefully acknowledged that "nine-tenths of the
> applause is due Mr. Thayer," at the same time
> looking toward that part of the theater where the
> latter gentleman was seated.
>
> The pleasant little episode was in the nature
> of a surprise to some in the audience, who had
> not known before of Mr. Thayer's authorship, in
> like manner with Mr. Hopper himself. Mr. Hopper
> will be Mr. Thayer's guest at dinner today, with
> other friends.

Also in the audience that night was the Worcester
Gazette reporter. He gives the few words with which Hopper
introduced his *Casey* performance, which came apparently
as a curtain-call at the end of *WANG* after the applause had

died down. "Ladies and gentlemen," said Hopper stepping forward to the footlights, "I am going to throw in a little extra tonight. It is hardly Siamese, and perhaps it is a little incongruous but . . . I think you will be glad to hear it." Some years before, he went on, he'd run across "something which I have clung to ever since, and which has done more to win me applause than anything else in my repertoire" (an exaggeration, of course, meant as a compliment to the listening Thayer). He then made his mention of the poem's author being in the audience, and launched into his recital.

The dinner held prior to *WANG*'s second performance took place at the Worcester Club, and was notable for one incident. After the plates had been cleared away, though it took some persuading, Thayer was induced to recite his famous ballad (that is, *read* it, since he certainly would not at that time have had it by heart). His low, soft, droning voice gave the lively lines little dramatic emphasis, and Hopper—quite unreasonably!—was sorely disappointed. "It was terrible," he later wrote as if judging a fellow actor. "That man had no idea, absolutely no idea, none at all, of how that poem should be recited!"

With a small party of his friends, Thayer was also at the second performance, occupying a private box. Afterwards they all went back to the club where, as the Worcester *Telegram* reported next morning, "many members of the club were present, and the prince of singing comedians charmed them with his funny stories and recitations. The party was altogether informal."

Thayer had already congratulated Hopper on his stage rendition of the poem. Now, after Thayer had heard it twice,

Ernest L. Thayer at about age fifty, when he was running the family Woolen mills. (Below) Thayer at age seventy-one in a photo taken at his 50th Harvard class reunion in 1935.

the comedian was eager to hear the author's opinion more frankly, and in detail. At some point that evening he must have asked Thayer about it point blank: did Mr. Thayer think that his rather broad interpretation—a bit exaggerated, emphatic—was right for such a ballad? Probably Thayer would have given an honest reply. If he did, how might *that* conversation have gone?

"Don't be shy, now, I really do want to hear what you think. If there's a way to improve my presentation I want to hear it! Some few people have already suggested to me that I might tone down a little what they call my overblown style. Soften it, so to speak. Give it more in the way of normal talk."

"No! Not at all!" objected Thayer. "It's perfect the way you do it now. Invigorates the picture. Animates it. What I heard on the stage tonight was a revelation to me. You have found more in that little poem than I ever thought I'd built into it! You put flesh on bare bones!"

Hopper beamed. "I knew I had it right! Doing a poem—a script!—like that on a stage in a big, crowded hall, the appeal has to be a lot broader, more theatrical. Doing it in a serious, literary way would fall flat every time. It's a *comic* turn, and all depends on the voice."

"Yes! The wonderful way you use your voice to suggest different meanings, and people, and situations . . . a rare balance of the real and the imaginary. That's genius! No, don't change a thing."

As the two parted that night, Thayer handed Hopper an envelope. In it, he said, were a couple of his other poems that the actor might like. As Hopper found, they were entitled "The Puritan Maid" and "The Detective." All Hopper ever said about them was this off-hand comment: "These I recited also, and I believe they were published. Oh, they were funny, very humorous indeed." Neither has ever been traced. Nor has any record been found of Hopper reciting any Thayer poem but *Casey*.

Remarkably, within four years of that meeting of the two, because of widespread reprinting in newspapers and magazines, and Hopper's public recitals, *Casey* had gained national attention. Before the century ran out it was being hailed by *The Sporting News* as "a baseball classic . . . [we] make it a point to serve it up for our readers once a year, and requests for copies of it come in at all seasons and from all quarters." Requests for back numbers of the magazine containing the poem came regularly "from all parts of the country."

At one point in 1896 the poem's growing fame almost lured Thayer back into journalism. In that year the *Examiner* in San Francisco, in which the poem had originally appeared sixteen years before, was so impressed by its burgeoning success that the paper's owner, William Randolph Hearst himself, invited Thayer to return to the coast with full freedom to write whatever he liked for the *Examiner*, prose or verse. Thayer declined. Then Hearst dangled a similar post on his New York paper, *The Journal*, with a bigger salary. Reluctant but intrigued, this time Thayer accepted.

Going down to New York—not so far away from Worcester that he couldn't easily return for frequent visits—he remained for some three months, writing regularly, including several ballads. Then, perhaps inevitably, he again decided that journalism wasn't for him. Back he went to Worcester.

The best of his *Journal* ballads, he thought, was one

titled "Murphy's Pig," a political jibe exposing the faults of a prominent New York official. But, as he confessed, "it did not catch on," and a similar fate met his other verse productions, all of them "doomed to the quick oblivion that meets newspaper verse."

The sad truth, of course, is that Thayer's talent as a poet, thin to start with and never fully at his command, had finally dribbled away, and with it went all his early literary ambition. That fact makes more wonderful—and more puzzling—his creation of that one inspired ballad which certainly did *not* meet a "quick oblivion."

For some years just before and just after the turn of the century Thayer had to bear the considerable annoyance of having strangers attempt to steal his creation, making spurious claims of authorship. Because he'd signed the poem in the *Examiner* only with the nickname "Phin," and never afterwards bothered about it, not even in its frequent reprintings, he'd left the way open for pretenders. Four or five of them, out of a dozen or more, actually gained a hearing, their stories backed by much fanciful detail. Mostly at first, the disgusted Thayer ignored the situation, but finally agreed to talk when approached by *Baseball Magazine* wanting to settle the question.

"The claims to authorship of *Casey*," declared Thayer with a sigh of resignation, "multiply throught the years, and I am getting a little tired of the subject. I have heard of as many as three in as many weeks." One claimant he'd found so aggravating in his bold distortions, "that I employed a Pinkerton detective to look into the matter. It is simply impossible to stop this kind of thievery."

Fully expecting that it would finally put the question to rest, he gave *Baseball Magazine* a full account of his writing of the poem. It made no difference. The authorship argument went merrily on, leading another popular magazine of the day, *The Scrap Book*, to take up the chase.

Hiring a recognized scholar, Harry Thurston Peck, to conduct a serious study of the dispute, the magazine directed him to "follow up every possible clue, and go to first-hand sources." Taking several months to finish, Peck did a thorough job, and his report appeared in *The Scrap Book* for December 1908. As well as a sworn affidavit from Thayer himself, it featured testimony on Thayer's behalf by several old *Examiner* staffers who'd known the poet well. After sifting all the evidence on all claimants, Peck concluded that Ernest L. Thayer, of Worcester, Massachusetts, was certainly the poem's sole and true author, a judgment he expressed as undoubtedly "beyond all question."

The hot dispute over *Casey*'s authorship, proudly declared *The Scrap Book*, had been settled, completely and finally. But it hadn't. Every year or two during ensuing decades some eager editor would again loudly demand "Who wrote *Casey at the Bat*!" By then the disinterested author had given up replying to such inquiries.

Thankfully, the Thayer story has a happy ending.

In 1913 at age fifty, after he'd spent another decade of leisure, often wandering around Europe with long periods of residence in Florence—and twenty-five years after his devastating encounter with the heartless Miss Lent—Thayer at last married. While visiting in southern California he met a charming young widow, Rosalind Hammett. That September

Ernest Thayer with his wife Rosalind. The photo was made in 1913 the year of their marriage, when Thayer was fifty years old. He had suffered an earlier love disappointment, in the same year that he wrote Casey.

the two were wed, and after a lengthy honeymoon in Japan they went to live in a big house by the sea in Montecito, a suburb of Santa Barbara.

There, on August 21, 1940, the modest author of *Casey at the Bat*, aged seventy-seven, died of a stroke.

Not until 1906 did the Victor Company put Hopper's recital of *Casey* on a record. By then he'd been reciting it regularly for fifteen years, and the fast-growing record industry had been in full swing for well over a decade. *Casey* had reached the zenith of its fame, as had Hopper's recital of it, so the question naturally arises: why did Victor take so long to get around to it?

The answer is obvious, reflecting an attitude common then among performing artists. He didn't want to give away all at once, in effect to kill the specialty number that was working so well for him in person on the stage.

The 1906 recording, he was relieved to find, while a huge success, didn't at all interfere with his personal use of the poem. When it was re-issued in 1913 it was backed by Bell giving his own humorous rendition of a *Casey* take-off: "The Man Who Fanned Casey." In 1926, using Victor's new, much-advertised "orthophonic" process, Hopper re-cut *Casey*, and the record went right on selling in large quantities. With these commercial uses of his ballad Thayer had no connection. He'd meant it when, at their 1892 meeting, he generously gave Hopper full and unlimited rights to the poem.

Despite the popularity of his *Casey* recording, however, disappointments did come to Hopper in connection with the ballad. The sorriest was his attempt in 1916 to go the final step and take it to Hollywood, which failed miserably. Film was silent then, depriving him of his knock-out talent as a comic singer, so perhaps the effort was doomed from the start. The film—of course entitled *Casey at the Bat*—was presented as a serious love story, climaxing with the Mudville baseball game. Casey's strikeout isn't his own fault, but comes as a result of his being distracted at the critical moment by an incident in the stands. The dour review of the picture that appeared in *Variety* told it all: the famous poem "made a corking subject for a comedy picture," but unfortunately had come out as "a cheap, mushy heart-thriller." The 53-year-old Hopper had been badly miscast, had "failed utterly to look the part," on top of which he'd "acted extremely badly."

It was not only *Casey* who'd struck out in this first attempt to flesh out and film the ballad. Hopper whiffed, too, Hollywood giving up on the still popular but aging stage star.

As for Hopper's passing—on September 23, 1935—it too was linked to *Casey* and baseball. Let the New York *Times* tell of his final moments:

> . . . a strange rounding out of fate appeared in the actor's last words, which referred to his interest in baseball, the subject of his most famous recitation, "Casey at the Bat."
>
> At eleven o'clock last night Mr. Hopper had insisted on sitting up in bed to smoke a pipe while he looked over the sports pages of a newspaper. Physicians insisted that he needed a rest, and tried to persuade him to go to sleep. But he

waved them aside with a characteristic gesture.

"See you tomorrow, Doc," he said. "I never sleep until 3 A.M. anyway. Run along while I see what the Cards (the St. Louis National League team) did."

Shortly after dawn a nurse noticed that Mr. Hopper appeared to be having trouble drawing his breath. She called an intern. When he arrived the patient was dead.

It was his heart.

The funeral was held in the actor's own chapel at 29th Street, The Little Church Around the Corner. In the crowd of more than a thousand mourners that filled the small building, said the *Times*, there could be spotted stage celebrities galore, "many present-day luminaries of Broadway, and many more dating as far back as the Mauve Decade, whose fame has faded."

Thirty honorary pall-bearers followed the casket. Six of them were fellow actors who remembered Hopper from the Eighties, themselves now hallowed names (David Warfield, William Gillette, Joe Weber, Lew Fields, Daniel Frohman, and Francis Wilson, who'd played with Hopper in that funny benefit game almost a half-century before).

Also in the line of honorary pall-bearers was George M. Cohan, whose first sight of Hopper went back to *WANG* in the early Nineties.

EXIT MUSIC

MEMORIALS

T EN DAYS AFTER IT HAD REPORTED THE DEATH OF CASEY'S
author, the New York *Times* carried a story about a serious proposal to commemorate Ernest Thayer's unique
contribution to the game. Made by a leading baseball execu-
tive, it offered no small or inconspicuous idea, calling for the
setting of the entire poem, all fifty-two lines, in bronze:

THAYER MEMORIAL URGED

BASEBALL TRIBUTE TO AUTHOR OF
'CASEY AT THE BAT' PROPOSED

Washington, Aug. 30 (AP)—Clark Griffith,
President of the Senators, and a vice-president of
the American league, suggested today that organized baseball erect a memorial to Ernest L.
Thayer, author of "Casey at the Bat." Thayer
died last week in Santa Barbara, Calif.

"The memorial," Griffith said, "should be
large enough to include every stanza of the poem

that has meant as much to baseball as anything I can think of." The president of the Senators said he would present his suggestion at the next meeting of the American League.

In the meantime, he said, he plans to take up the matter of the memorial with executives of organized baseball. Griffith said he had no ideas about where the memorial should be erected, and would welcome suggestions from fans as well as baseball men.

"Casey at the Bat," said Griffith, "has been a fine, wholesome factor in promoting our national pastime and I think we should do something to perpetuate the poem and the man who wrote it."

Nothing happened. Nor has Griffith's generous and eminently fitting proposal ever been renewed.

In the United States Congress, on June 3, 1988, all eyes turned to Rep. Tom Lantos of Los Angeles as he rose and asked to be recognized. Most of the members were already aware that the day marked *Casey*'s centenary.

"Mr. Speaker," Lantos began, his tone solemn, "in this hallowed hall, in this historic building, we commemorate events of great significance for our nation and for the American people. Today, Mr. Speaker, I call the attention of my distinguished colleagues to the centennial of the publication of one of the best-known works in American literature—I refer, of course to . . . 'Casey at the Bat" [which] first appeared one hundred years ago today in the San Francisco *Examiner.*" Employing a little of the same humorous exaggeration found in the poem, he went on:

> Baseball, Mr. Speaker, is one of the highlights of American culture, one of America's greatest contributions to world civilization. As the former President of the United States, Herbert Hoover, said, "Next to religion, baseball has furnished a greater impact on American life than any other institution . . ."
>
> On this auspicious anniversary, the lyric strains of "Casey at the Bat" should be included in the record of this day's proceedings so that my colleagues may reflect on its profound sentiments.

No objection being heard, pronounced the Speaker, it was so ordered. In its entirety, *Casey at the Bat* now appears in the *Congressional Record*, Vol. 1988, page H3962-63.

Some dozen years after that came another honor, one that fittingly and for all time linked the poem and its popularizer.

In 2002, Hopper's ninety-six-year-old recording of *Casey* (made in 1906) was chosen for inclusion in the National Recording Registry (equivalent to that for national landmarks). Administered by the Library of Congress, the Registry selects for honored preservation recordings "that are culturally, historically, or aesthetically important, and/or inform or reflect life in the United States."

No more satisfying ending for the story of Hopper and *Casey* can be imagined (anyway, in the opinion of one admirer,

Ho

Honeymooning (Poulton)	Stevenson and Stanley	16014 10
Sailing—Old Sea Song (Marks)	Hayden Quartet	

Honeymoon Express—See "My Yellow Jacket Girl" and
"Spaniard That Blighted My Life"

Honeymooning, Honey, in Bombay (Reed)	"That Girl" Qt	16703 10
Slip on Your Gingham Gown (Berris-Smith)	Collins and Harlan	
Honeymoon March (Rosey) Ocarina Solo	Mosé Tapiero	52020 10
Honeymoon, The (Kiburz) Piccolo John F. Kiburz and Pryor's B		17074 10
Cousinchen Waltz (Hollaender) Whistling	Guido Gialdini	
Honey, Won't You Please Come Down	Collins and Harlan	16513 10
Who ? Me ? (Snyder)	Collins and Harlan	
Honor and Arms—Samson (Handel)	Herbert Witherspoon	74070 12

HOOLEY, WILLIAM F., Bass

Asleep in the Deep (Petrie) and Larboard Watch—Macdonough and Hooley		16949 10
Larboard Watch—with Macdonough and Asleep in the Deep (Petrie) Hooley		16949 10
Rolling Stone (Botsford) with Qt and That Mysterious Rag—American Qt		16982 10
When the Rainbow Shines—with Cho and Tenn. Moon—Heidelberg Qt		17207 10
Hoop-e-Kack—Two-Step (Jacobs) Xylophone	W. H. Reitz	17265 10
Medley—"Little Bit of Everything" Banjo	Vess L. Ossman	

HOPPER, DE WOLF, Comedian

Mr. Hopper has been persuaded to make us a record of his famous and immortal baseball classic, and it is the most perfect reproduction of the comedian's eccentric delivery which could be imagined. Shut your eyes and you can imagine the whole scene—five thousand of Mudville's fans yelling for their favorite—the redoubtable and mighty Casey standing proudly at the bat—the pitcher gripping the ball —then a moment of hushed expectancy—and then . . . and then the tragedy begins!

HOPPER

Let us draw the veil—suffice to say that you can actually feel the breeze on your face when the great Casey fans the air as he strikes out! Mr. Hopper record of his celebrated baseball recitation has made one of the biggest hits in Victor history

RECORDS BY MR. HOPPER

Casey at the Bat—Humorous Base Ball Recitation	Thayer	31559 12 1.0
Casey at the Bat and Man Who Fanned Casey—A reply—Digby Bell		35290 12 1

HORN—ENGLISH and FRENCH—For examples of these instruments see "Educational"

HORNPIPES

Favorite Hornpipe Medley and Medley of Old Reels—Violin—D'Almaine		16393 10
Hornpipe Medley—Kimmel Accordion and Three Solitaires—Cornets-Trombone		16317 10
Hortense at Sea Humorous Monologue	Nat M. Wills	35093 12
Tale of the Cheese Humorous Monologue	Murry K. Hill	
Hortense at the Skating Rink Monologue	Nat M. Wills	35156 12 1
Uncle Josh Keeps House	Cal Stewart	
Hosanna—Easter Song (Granier)	Herbert Witherspoon	74279 12
Hosanna (Easter Song) (Jules Granier) In French	Enrico Caruso	88403 12 3.0
Hosanna (Granier)	Harry Macdonough	16060 10
Holy Night—Noël (Adam)	Harry Macdonough	
Hot Tamale Man (Ingraham)	Arthur Collins	16293 10
Uncle Josh and the Billiken	Cal Stewart	
Hour of Love, The (McDonnell-Weymann)	Fred'k Wheeler	17275 10
When I Lost You (Irving Berlin)	Henry Burr	
Hour That Gave Me You, The (Schmid)	Arthur Clough	17017 10
A Girlie Was Just Made to Love (Meyer)	Walter Van Brunt	
How Can They Tell That Oi'm Irish (Norworth)	Nora Bayes	70030 12
How Columbus Discovered America Eccentric Monologue		16890 10
	Murry K. Hill	
Village Barber—Specialty (Banjo by Van Eps)	Porter and Harlan	
How Firm a Foundation (Keith-Portugallo)	Trinity Choir	16674
Face to Face (Herbert Johnson)	Percy Hemus	

The Victor Record Company catalogue of 1913 gave special attention to DeWolf Hopper's 1906 recording of Casey, including a portrait of the actor. The record, it said, was "one of the biggest hits" in its then quarter-century of business. On the same page are mentioned Irving Berlin, Nora Bayes, and Enrico Caruso.

who has spent many delighted hours listening to his daring and evocative vocal artistry) than the advertising blurb for that 1906 recording. It appeared in the Victor catalogue at the time and—except for a single misapplied word—told only the truth:

> Mr. Hopper has been persuaded to make us a record of his famous and immortal baseball classic, and it is the most perfect reproduction of the comedian's eccentric delivery which could be imagined. Shut your eyes and you can imagine the whole scene—
>
> Five thousand of Mudville's fans yelling for their favorite—the redoubtable and mighty Casey standing proudly at the bat—the pitcher gripping the ball—then a moment of hushed expectancy— and then . . . and then the tragedy begins!
>
> Let us draw the veil—suffice it to say that you can actually feel the breeze on your face when the great Casey fans the air as he strikes out! Mr. Hopper's record of this celebrated baseball recitation has made one of the biggest hits in Victor history.

Eccentric, did he say? Hopper's style in bringing the immortal tale alive is *eccentric*?

Never!

It's pure genius, right on the nose!

APPENDIX A

FIRST PUBLICATION OF
CASEY AT THE BAT

FOLLOWING IS THE ORIGINAL PRINTING OF THE POEM IN facsimile, enlarged from the San Francisco *Examiner*, Sunday, June 3, 1888, page 4. The way many of the lines have been broken to run over—several breaking a word in half—show that Thayer's original form was long-line quatrains, much too wide for the paper's narrow-column format. Probably Thayer used the long-line style because that's the way the *Bab Ballads* of W.S. Gilbert were written (for more on Gilbert's influence see p. 44).

CASEY AT THE BAT.

A Ballad of the Republic, Sung in the Year 1888.

The outlook wasn't brilliant for the Mudville
    nine that day;
The score stood four to two with but one in-
    ning more to play.

And then when Cooney died at first, and Bar-
    rows did the same,
A sickly silence fell upon the patrons of the
    game.

A straggling few got up to go in deep despair.
    The rest
Clung to that hope which springs eternal in the
    human breast;
They thought if only Casey could but get a
    whack at that—
We'd put up even money now with Casey at the
    bat.

But Flynn preceded Casey, as did also Jimmy
    Blake,
And the former was a lulu and the latter was a
    cake;
So upon that stricken multitude grim mel-
    ancholy sat,
For there seemed but little chance of Casey's get-
    ting to the bat.

But Flynn let drive a single, to the wonderment
    of all,
And Blake, the much despis-ed, tore the cover
    off the ball;
And when the dust had lifted, and the men saw
    what had occurred,
There was Johnnie safe at second and Flynn
    a-hugging third. *

Then from 5,000 throats and more there rose a
    lusty yell;
It rumbled through the valley, it rattled in the
    dell;

---

* Johnnie is a compositor's error for the *Jimmy* in line 10, and
missed by the proofreader.

It knocked upon the mountain and recoiled upon
    the flat,
For Casey, mighty Casey, was advancing to the
    bat.

There was ease in Casey's manner as he stepped
    into his place;
There was pride in Casey's bearing and a smile
    on Casey's face.
And when, responding to the cheers, he lightly
    doffed his hat,
No stranger in the crowd could doubt 'twas
    Casey at the bat.

Ten thousand eyes were on him as he rubbed
    his hands with dirt;
Five thousand tongues applauded when he
    wiped them on his shirt.
Then while the writhing pitcher ground the ball
    into his hip,
Defiance gleamed in Casey's eye, a sneer curled
    Casey's lip.

And now the leather-covered sphere came
    hurtling through the air,
And Casey stood a-watching it in haughty
    grandeur there.
Close by the sturdy batsman the ball unheeded
    sped—
"That ain't my style," said Casey. "Strike
    one," the umpire said.

From the benches, black with people, there went
    up a muffled roar,
Like the beating of the storm-waves on a stern
    and distant shore.
"Kill him! Kill the umpire!" shouted some
    one on the stand;

And it's likely they'd have killed him had not
 Casey raised his hand.

With a smile of Christian charity great Casey's
 visage shone;
He stilled the rising tumult; he bade the game
 go on;
He signaled to the pitcher, and once more the
 spheroid flew;
But Casey still ignored it, and the umpire said,
 "Strike two."

"Fraud!" cried the maddened thousands, and
 echo answered fraud;
But one scornful look from Casey and the audience was awed.
They saw his face grow stern and cold, they saw
 his muscles strain,
And they knew that Casey wouldn't let that ball
 go by again.

The sneer is gone from Casey's lip, his teeth are
 clinched in hate;
He pounds with cruel violence his bat upon the
 plate.
And now the pitcher holds the ball, and now he
 lets it go,
And now the air is shattered by the force of
 Casey's blow.

Oh, somewhere in this favored land the sun is
 shining bright;
The band is playing somewhere, and somewhere
 hearts are light,
And somewhere men are laughing, and somewhere children shout;
But there is no joy in Mudville—mighty Casey
 has struck out.   —PHIN.

APPENDIX B

THAYER'S PHRASING

A NYONE READING THROUGH CONTEMPORARY ACCOUNTS OF 1888 baseball games, as I have done in some half-dozen different newspapers, will hear constant strong echoes of *Casey*'s vocabulary and phrasing. Often they match Thayer's exact words or come close to it. I have not tried to track all of the poem's thirty or so examples—the few I caught have been accidental—but have no doubt that it can be done, given a good deal of patient searching.

The standard baseball reporting style of the time was quite distinctive, having an added charm all its own—a bit tongue-in-cheek, a bit consciously humorous and satirical, more than a bit elevated and formal, even "literary." It is this special air or atmosphere that Thayer has so well captured in *Casey*, and which makes his poem unique, a perfectly lit, perfectly focused photograph of old-time, yet timeless, baseball. His deft and loving use of the day's sportswriting jargon is what works the magic.

A list of the special phrases Thayer lifted from newspapers may be of interest, at least for readers inclined to keep an eye peeled when looking at old accounts of nineteenth-century games. The first four examples in the list are mentioned in my text above (p. 49), with their newspaper equivalents.

I should add that the pivotal phrase in the second stanza—"that hope which springs eternal in the human breast"—I do not include in the list because I have a nagging feeling that I've encountered it before, in some pre-Casey writing, non-baseball. I have not found it, or anything near it, in game accounts (except for the one instance mentioned above on page 137, which I attribute to Thayer's influence). If I'm wrong, and the effective phrase is Thayer's own, I profusely apologize to the poet.

The order of the phrases listed here follows that of their appearance in the poem. The numbers identify the stanza:

1. outlook wasn't brilliant
   died at first
   sickly silence
   patrons of the game

2. get a whack at that

3. stricken multitude
   grim melancholy

4. wonderment of all
   tore the cover off the ball
   a-huggin' third

5. advancing to the bat

6. ease in Casey's manner
   lightly doffed his hat

7. tongues applauded
   the writhing pitcher
   defiance gleamed

8. leather-covered sphere
   haughty grandeur
   sturdy batsman

9. benches black with people

    beating of the storm
    waves on a stern and
    distant shore

    "Kill the umpire!"

10. visage shone
    rising tumult
    the spheroid flew

11. maddened thousands
    echo answered
    one scornful look
    grow stern and cold

12. cruel violence
    air is shattered

13. favored land
    no joy in

The 13th and final stanza perfectly echoes the mock, world-ending despair often to be met in the concluding paragraphs of actual game reports in the newspapers of the 1880s. Aside from the two phrases listed here for the last stanza, I'm inclined to think it is Thayer's original work. In particular I credit him with that subtly effective, fivefold use of the heartbreaking "somewhere," each repetition of which a little further tightens the screw. (In Hopper's stage version the five "somewheres" are placed a bit differently to heighten the rhetorical impact.) My choice for Thayer's most subtly original touch in the poem would have to be that sneaky-clever image in stanza 7, lines 3 & 4, offering perfect if loving satire. A batter rubbing his hands with dirt to get a better grip on the bat was a common act then and until long after. But only Thayer has the excited crowd vocally admire the familiar procedure:

Ten thousand eyes were on him
    As he rubbed his hands with dirt;
Five thousand tongues applauded
    When he wiped them on his shirt.

PROGRAM NOTES

MINGLED HERE ARE SOURCE CITATIONS AND SOME DISCUS-
sion of matters treated or mentioned in the text.
Sources are cited in short form and may be identified
by a glance at the bibliography. Down the left-hand margin
are displayed *page* numbers.

13   "When my name is"—Hopper, *Clown*, 72. Referring
to his first recital of *Casey* in 1888 at Wallack's
Theater, he comments, "No bronze memorial tablet
marks the site, yet the day may come. Lesser events
have been so commemorated." The theater is long
since gone, and no tablet marks the site.

16   "The biggest baseball crank"—Chicago *Tribune*,
Aug. 15, 1888. When he died, in 1935, Hopper was
reading newspaper accounts of the previous day's
games.

16   "at the Polo Grounds"—Hopper, *Clown*, 76.

18   "He is as perennial"—Russell, *Cosmopolitan*, 110. The closest connection between Hopper and Lillian Russell came in the Nineties, when both performed in the Weber and Fields troupe.

23   *Giants home opener of 1888*: New York *Times* and *Tribune*, both for April 26, 1888. Hopper's friendship with Mutrie and the Giant players is mentioned in his *Clown*, 76.

31   *Plot of Lady or the Tiger*: Norton 467-68; Ganzl 109-11, New York *Times* and *Evening Post*, both May 8, 1888. 'The Lady or the Tiger?', by Frank R. Stockton.

33   *The Boston—New York Series*: New York *Times*, April 30-May 4, 1888.

35   "a feature of the game"—New York *Times*, May 4, 1888.

37   *67 Chatham Street*: Moore/Vermilyea, 15. The Thayer home was "a substantial but not extravagant residence . . . in the Greek Revival style." It had separate rooms for music and billiards, and a library. It was pulled down in 1967.

38   *San Francisco Examiner*: Thayer's eighteen-month career on this paper, owned by his Harvard classmate, William Randolph Hearst, is well covered in Moore/Vermilyea 178-229.

40   "writing for a living"——Moore/Vermilyea, 188. The remark is quoted in a letter by his sister. In a later letter from San Francisco, Thayer adds: "It

would not perhaps be such a colossal misfortune if I did turn out a failure in journalistic walks . . . the work becomes continuously more exhausting and difficult." (200)\

41 *Thayer's love disappointment*: All that is known of the episode is in the letters between Thayer and his family, in Moore/Vermilyea, 189, 193, 207, 214. These strongly suggest that the loss of Miss Lent was his real reason for leaving San Francisco and going home.

42 "Never before in the"—quoted from the *Examiner* in Moore/Vermilyea, 196.

42 ". . . has inaugurated"—quoted from the *Examiner* in Moore/Vermilyea, 204.

43 *The Connor home run*: Moore/Vermilyea, 222. Shortly after this, Connor went back east and the San Francisco *Chronicle* commented: "Our local twirlers heaved a great sigh of relief when they learned that Roger Connor had packed his grip and stolen silently away."

43 "with a generous burst"—quoted from the *Examiner* in Moore/Vermilyea, 224.

44 *Thayer and the Bab Ballads*: Croy, 11 (1908 interview with Thayer). The ballads appeared in book form at intervals, beginning in 1877. The Gilbert Preface appeared in all editions.

46 "decided I could do"—Croy 11. Thayer adds: "I wrote a poem for each Sunday edition of the

Examiner for three months." That would mean a dozen poems, not including *Casey*. Six of the dozen are printed in whole or in part in Gardner, 199-204. The longest, "A Sea Ballad," is an obvious takeoff on Gilbert's "The Yarn of the Nancy Bell," best known of the *Bab* ballads.

46   "I evolved Casey from"—Croy, 11. Of the four Mudville players named in the poem aside from Casey, the names of two of them (Cooney and Flynn) match players on the minor-league California team at Stockton, near San Francisco (Moore/Vermilyea, 234-35).

47   "There was a great buzz"— New York *Herald*, Aug. 19, 1888. Same for the next quote.

47   "The score was in New"—New York *Times*, Aug. 2, 1888.

47   "What a hub-bub"—New York *Herald*, Aug 19, 1888.

47   *Background for Connor and Kelly*: personal sources on Connor are few and scattered. Much more has been written on Kelly, including a short biography, that by Appel, but concentrating on his baseball career. There is also Kelly's own book, a casual autobiography published at the start of the 1888 season: *Play Ball: Stories of the Diamond Field*, the first of the sports celebrity books.

54   ". . . he was a creator"—quoted in Appel, 96.

55   *Kelly's attempted steal of home*: this happened in the

Chicago-Boston game of May 28, 1885. According to the New York *Clipper*, "Kelly made an audacious but futile attempt to tie the score by running in from third while the ball was being pitched to the catcher, who was standing close up to the plate."(Clipper, Feb. 26, 1887, 793)

56   "His policy has always"—New York *Clipper*, Feb. 26, 1887, 793. The article goes on to list some of Kelly's feats. In a game against New York on Sept. 29, 1885, he went 5 for 5 with three triples. In 1885 he scored 124 runs off 126 hits. During seven years with Chicago he played in 675 games, got 890 hits, on which he scored 727 runs. Of course that only begins to list his accomplishments on the field.

56   "Ray slammed a whistling"—New York *Herald*, Aug 18, 1888.

60   "big, dour, Irish lad"—from a letter written by Thayer on Jan. 11, 1930 in reply to a question from the Syracuse *Post-Standard*, quoted in full in Moore/Vermilyea, 315. The Dan Casey in question was not a baseball player. He became a teacher in the Worcester public schools, eventually principal of the Grafton Street School, and died in 1915. His niece described him as "a gentle giant of a man." (Boston *Globe* Oct 10, 1978). In his letter to the *Post-Standard*, Thayer states firmly that "the poem has no basis in fact," meaning no specific game or incident or personality. This has not prevented any number of men from claiming to be the original of

the Mudville hero, all of whom have been rejected or are obviously not qualified. The topic long since became tiresome, but can be followed in Murdock, 22-30, and Moore/Vermilyea, 275-80.

63   "There is no doubt"—quoted from the *Examiner* in Moore/Vermilyea, 22.

64   ". . . is as perfect an"—Hopper, *Clown*, 93.

64   *Thayer's pseudonym*: satisfied to sign his poems "Phin," at first the easy-going Thayer made no effort to substitute his real name or to establish his authorship of *Casey*. As a result the inevitable false claimants quickly appeared, at one time totaling a half-dozen. At last, as the debate grew serious, Thayer took a hand, still rather casual, and his authorship was publicly proved beyond all doubt. For some brief treatment of a matter which is now of little interest, see above, 157. Murdock 9-21, and Moore/Vermilyea, 286-301, give fuller detail.

An interesting sidelight is provided on Thayer by one of his Harvard *Lampoon* colleagues, the late philosopher George Santayana, in a brief mention in his 1944 autobiography (*Persons and Places*, p. 189). Remarkably, Santayana shows no knowledge of Thayer's subsequent career, not even that he'd written a widely loved poem. "The man who gave the tone to the *Lampoon*" wrote Santayana, "was Ernest Thayer . . . he seemed a man apart, and his wit was not so much jocular as Mercutio-like, curious and whimsical, as if he saw the broken edges of things that appear whole, and a feeling. . . that the absurd side of things was pathetic. Probably nothing in his later performance may bear out what I have said of him, because American life was becoming unfavourable to idiosyncracies of any sort." How did Santayana get through life without discovering that his admired old schoolmate was author of the country's most famous serio-comic ballad? One thing is certain: the philosopher was no baseball fan!

68   "I never read a libretto"—New York *Times*, April 1, 1888. The second interview with McCaull appeared on April 29.

69   *The question answered*: rather unfairly, the New York *Evening Post* on May 8, 1888 gave away the play's answer to the question of which came out of the door, the lady or the tiger.

73   "very wearisome"—New York *Evening Post*, May 8, 1888.

73   "a very amusing solution"—New York *Times*, May 8, 1888. Unlike the *Post*, the *Times* did not give away the solution.

73   "DeWolf Hopper as"—New York *Times*, May 8, 1888.

74   "were being whistled"—New York *Times*, May 13, 1888. "The advance sales for the next two weeks," added the paper, "are extremely large, and the clever comic opera promises to have a long run."

74   *The horse-racing verse*: Quoted in New York *World*,

May 23, 1888 as a sample of the several horse-racing verses interpolated in the show. This was a practice of the operetta scene at the time.

75　*Decoration Day doubleheader*: New York *Times*, May 31, 1888.

76　"Formed a horseshoe"—New York *Times*, May 31, 1888.

76　*Attendance figures*: New York *Times*, May 24, 1888. The story adds: "A potpurri of the principal airs of the piece will be published next week by a well-known firm," of course as sheet music. The firm was Witmark's.

77　*Connor's home run*: New York *Times*, May 31, 1888. It was a line-shot to right-center that easily cleared the high fence, still rising as it went over.

77　*Chicago team dress-coats*: New York *Times*, June 8, 1888. Next day when Chicago repeated the joke, the Giants were ready for them, taking the field "attired in long linen dusters, the tails of which were cut in the shape of claw-hammer coats. Every man wore a tall white hat. . . . They marched to the grandstand and after lifting their hats made a neat salaam, took off their coats and hats and started to practice amid roars of laughter." (New York *Times*, June 10, 1888.)

77　". . . looked as though"—New York *Herald*, June 13, 1888.

78　"His magnificent throw"—Chicago *Tribune*, June 9, 1888.

78 "Time and again men were"—New York *Times*, June 13, 1888.

79 "The members of the McCaull"—New York *Times*, July 3, 1888.

62 *A.C. Gunter*: The only source for Gunter's crucial part in the *Casey* story is Hopper himself, in *Clown*, 77. Gunter, he says, "saw the announcement [in the papers] and looked up McCaull at once. 'I've got just the thing for your baseball night,' Gunter told him. 'It's a baseball poem I cut out of a Frisco paper when I was on the coast last winter. I've been carrying it around ever since. It's a lulu and young Hopper could do it to a turn.' Gunter had the clipping with him, and handed it over. McCaull read it, slapped his knee, and agreed." In error, of course, is that "last winter," the poem having appeared shortly before, on June 3rd.

For Gunter's personal background see *Cyclopedia of American Biography*, 247; *Cambridge Guide to the American Theater*, 460; *Dictionary of American Biography*, Vol. 8, 54; obituary, New York *Times*, Feb. 26, 1907. Gunter's turning his novel *Mr. Barnes* into a play is in the New York *Times*, Oct. 8, 1888. It debuted a week later at the Broadway Theater to generally bad reviews. It survived for several weeks, then went on tour. Worst was the *Times* notice, which called it "a dramatic monstrosity," adding that readers of the novel "fondly fabled that there could be nothing worse than that; but they had

not measured the possibilities of the stage," and . . .
but no! Wait! Stop! Because of Archie Gunter's
crucial, indeed pivotal role in the *Casey* saga he is
hereby pardoned for any and all literary faults and
shortcomings. Henceforth he is to be remembered
solely for his great insight and sure instinct in bringing the Thayer ballad to light.

85   "between Digby Bell, DeWolf"—Goodwin, 159.

86   "What would I not give"—Goodwin, 96-100. For
       further description and discussion of "The Rialto,"
       see McCabe, 571-79, Morris, 181-93, and Frick,
       passim. By the start of World War One the name had
       faded from use, especially after the theater district
       had moved further north, to 42nd Street.

98   "he was so heartily"—New York *Herald*, July 17,
       1888.

98   "was uproariously funny"—New York *Evening
       Post*, July 17, 1888.

98   "it was a brilliant piece"—Wilson, 66.

100 "his singing is so"—Leslie, *Players*, 563-65. The
       Hopper entry originally appeared in the Chicago
       Daily News in 1896 as a review of Sousa's *El
       Capitan*, starring Hopper.

100 "with a travesty of"—New York *Times*, July 31,
       1888. The New York *Herald* a few days later noted
       that "the take-off on the baseball clubs is a very
       popular feature and provokes unbounded laughter
       at every performance." (Aug. 5, 1888)

101   *The idea for a "Baseball Night"*—Hopper, *Clown*,
       gives this: "Bell and I suggested to Col. McCaull, for
       whom both of us were working, that a baseball
       night, with the White Stockings in one row of boxes,
       and the Giants in an opposite one, would be a happy
       idea for all hands, and he endorsed the suggestion."

       Some weeks before this a similar celebration for
       the city's winning baseball team had been held at
       Niblo's.

102   "Singers On the Ball Field"—New York *Herald*,
       Aug. 14, 1888. The same notice, sometimes short-
       ened and rewritten, appeared in most other New
       York papers.

102   "I've got a little item—Hopper, *Clown*, 77. Drawing
       on what Hopper says elsewhere I have slightly
       expanded his brief description of the incident.

103   *Hopper a quick study*: In *Clown*, 77-78, Hopper
       says that his memorizing of the poem was delayed
       by the sudden sickness of his young son at home in
       Onset Bay near Cape Cod. When a telegram brought
       word that the boy was all right, says Hopper, it was
       the very day of the "Baseball Night" at Wallack's
       and he memorized the poem in "less than an hour."
       But this is based on Hopper's error in dating the
       baseball night as May 14, not the actual August 14
       (he was writing some thirty-five years after the fact).
       Nor can the delay over his son be fitted into the
       known chronology of August. His ability as a
       "quick study" Hopper himself stresses (*Clown*, 79),
       as "a matter of gratitude with me rather than of

pride." While playing in Gilbert and Sullivan's *Iolanthe*, he claims, he memorized the long and wordy nightmare song in little more than an hour, which would be quite a feat.

104 *The Tally-Ho coaches*: McCabe, 258-64 (a contemporary description), and Morris, 149-50. Besides the regular runs, an annual "Coaching Day" was held on the last Saturday of May, when all the Tally-Hos would gather on Fifth Avenue and parade through Central Park and around the lower city, accompanied by liveried outriders and trumpet blasts, ending with a banquet at the Hotel Brunswick. Women passengers took care "to make the colors of their dresses harmonize with the prevailing tints of the coaches." (McCabe 263)

104 "If you were able to"—Morris, 150.

108 "Not only the two"—New York *Herald*, Aug. 15, 1888.

108 "While all this was"—New York *Herald*, Aug. 14, 1888.

109 "it came shortly, and"—New York *Times*, Aug. 14, 1888.

112 "They kept cheering"—New York *Times*, Aug. 15, 1888. Same for the paragraph's closing quote.

113 "The house was packed"—New York *World*, Aug. 15, 1888.

113 *Wallack's Theater*: McCabe, 572-77; Wallack, 24-27. *Harper's Weekly*, Nov. 1882. Wallack's "is one

of the most elegant and beautiful houses in the city. It was opened in 1881 and is . . . the favorite play-house with resident New Yorkers." (McCabe 577)

114 *General Sherman*: New York *World* and New York *Times*, both for Aug. 15, 1888. No biography of Sherman mentions his attendance at Wallack's that memorable night.

116 *Prince Methusalem*: for plot and background see Ganzl 186-88, Bordman, 163-64, and the original prompt books and dialogue parts at Mills Music Library, Univ. of Wisconsin, Madison.

116 *Prince Methusalem*, Act II, Scene 2: reconstructed here from the original vocal score, prompt books, and dialogue parts at the Mills Music Library, Madison, Wisc., Tams-Witmark Collection; see previous note.

118 *Lyrics for song, "The Dotlet On the I": —these* are quoted here from the original vocal score and prompt books—see previous two notes. For the 1888 Hopper production there would have been a new set of lyrics, but these have not survived.

122 *The baseball verses*: meant to suggest the tone and tenor of the originals, now lost, no doubt these samples don't measure up to those by Sydney Rosenfeld actually sung that night. My defense in presuming to write them is that, by way of the newsapers, I have been in the noisy crowd at almost every one of the 138 games played by the Giants that 1888 season!

123 "Ladies and gentlemen, since"—Hopper left no record of just how he introduced *Casey* that night, which came as an interruption to the flow of the operetta's action. Something very like what I picture here I think must have taken place.

124 *Hopper's recordings of* Casey: I am grateful to the Mills Music Library, Univ. of Wisconsin, Madison, for providing me with all three Hopper records of the poem on a single CD, which greatly facilitated my study of Hopper's unique style in the recitation. Interesting is the fact that the 1913 record is backed by Digby Bell reciting one of the many "replies" to the Thayer ballad, *The Man Who Fanned Casey*. His style is markedly different from Hopper's, more a standard declamation without verbal pyrotechnics, or any effort to dramatize.

131 "The first act of"—New York *Times*, Aug. 15, 1888.

132 "As might be expected"—New York *World*, Aug. 15, 1888.

132 "Hopper played the"—New York *Tribune*, Aug. 15, 1888.

135 "When it was evident"—New York *Times*, Aug. 16, 1888.

137 "as he walked up to the"—New York *Herald*, Aug. 16, 1888.

137 "The lamentations that"—New York *World*, Aug. 16, 1888.

137   "hope filled every breast"—New York *Herald*, Aug. 16, 1888. The phrase occurs when the Giants, behind 2-0, got two men aboard, with the hard—hitting Slattery coming up. But the hope in every Giant fan's breast lasted "only for a moment, for again Slattery was unequal to the emergency—his fly to Ryan left two on bases."

139   *The benefit game*: Hopper, *Clown*, 82-83, and New York *Times*, Sept. 8, 1888, which states that the game was "for the benefit of Carl Rankin, the dying minstrel," a victim of tuberculosis.

141   "WHAT CAN THE MATTER"—New York *World*, Aug. 31, 1888.

141   *The pennant-clinching game*: New York *Times* and Chicago *Tribune*, both for Oct. 5, 1888. It was, said the *Tribune*, "one of the most stubborn contests ever seen on a ball field. Brilliant plays abounded." In a game-saving catch, Anson "jumped fully four feet in the air and pulled down Tiernan's rising line drive." Ned Williamson, at short, "made a backward jumping catch of a liner that brought down the house."

144   *The pennant presentation*: New York *Times* and New York *Tribune*, both for Oct. 15, 1888. Formally attired, the entire Giant team stood on stage to receive the blue pennant.

144   *The 1888 World Series*: New York *Times*, Oct. 17-19; 23-26, 1888. In a private ceremony before game six Hopper and Bell were honored by the Giants with

the presentation of gold-headed canes (New York *World*, Oct 23, 1888, and Hopper, *Clown*, 76.).

145   "When Connor crossed the"—New York *World*, Oct. 23, 1888.

147   *King Kelly recites* Casey:— Moore/Vermilyea, 237-57; Appel, 128, 171.

150   *Death of Kelly*: obituaries in New York *Times*, and Chicago *Tribune*, both for Nov. 9, 1894. The personal comments of his friends are in the *Tribune* story, and in Boston *Globe*, Nov. 10, 1894.

151   ". . . too bad about Roger"—New York *Times*, Jan. 7, 1931. Judged on his career stats, taken relatively, Connor belongs among baseball's all-time top five hitters. On his retirement in 1897 he was the career leader in both home runs and triples, a combination never matched again, also walks. He was No. 2 in hits, runs, RBI, on-base percentage, total bases and slugging average. In BA he was No. 3, and in doubles No. 4. He was a truly unique talent.

153   "has achieved monumental"—New York *Times*, May 5, 1891.

156   "DeWolf Hopper has made"—New York *Post*, May 5, 1891.

156   "needed an added fillip"—Hopper, *Clown*, 84. The original prompt books for *WANG* are available at the Mills Music Library, Univ. of Wisconsin, Madison, but my careful look through them, some

half dozen, turned up no mention of *Casey*. Apparently it was sometimes used within the show, sometimes following the show.

157   "I never thought of"—Hopper, *Clown*, 84. Until he decided to use the poem regularly as part of *WANG*, Hopper would have felt no pressing need to identify the author. In a 1928 interview he told the Worcester *Daily Spy* (March 23, 1928) that he wrote to the *Examiner*, "But a great interval elapsed with no return word as to the identity and whereabouts of the author." Before an answer arrived, he'd accidentally met Thayer while playing Worcester in *WANG*.

157   *Hopper-Thayer meeting*: Hopper, *Clown*, 85-86; Worcester *Daily Spy*, Dec. 21, 1892, and Sept. 19, 1924; Worcester *Gazette*, Dec. 22, 1892. Lacking all detailed record of their conversation at this initial meeting, I feel that my suggested dialogue is justified—certainly they would have talked of *these* matters, at the least.

162   ". . . a noticeable incident"—Worcester *Daily Spy*, Dec. 21, 1892.

163   "Ladies and gentlemen, I"—Worcester *Gazette*, Dec. 22, 1892.

163   "it was terrible, that"—Worcester *Daily Spy*, March 23, 1928.

163   "Many members of the"—Worcester *Telegram*, Dec. 22, 1892. The story opens: "DeWolf Hopper delighted a crowded audience last night with his inimitable recitation of 'Casey At the Bat.' In a pri-

vate box sat Ernest. L. Thayer, a Worcester man and author of the poem."

166   "These I recited also"—Worcester *Daily Spy*, March 23, 1928. The titles of the two poems he gives in another interview in Worcester *Gazette*, Sept. 10, 1924. His recital of these unknown poems was probably done on private occasions.

166   *Thayer and the N.Y. Journal*: Croy, 12. The information as to Thayer's contributions to this paper came from Thayer himself in the interview.

167   "The claims to authorship"—Glenister, 53. Thayer adds: "I started on the trail of two other claimants, only to find that they had found refuge in the grave. If I can get hold of a live one who is a person of any consideration, I should like to make the beggar ashamed of himself."

168   "follow up every possible"—Peck, 947.

168   *Thayer's marriage and later life*: Moore/Vermilyea, 305-31, based on extensive research.

171   *Thayer's death*: New York *Times*, Aug. 22, 1940; Santa Barbara *News-Press*, Aug. 22, 1940.

171   "made a corking subject"—*Variety*, June 23, 1916. Though the picture fell short of expectations, guessed the paper, "the title will attract money," a salute to the poem's wide appeal.

171   "A strange rounding out"—New York *Times*, Sept. 24, 1935. Hopper had become ill, explained the paper, while serving as a narrator on a radio broad-

cast, and was taken to the hospital, where "seven hours later he was dead."

172   "many present day"— New York *Times*, Sept. 28, 1935. The account also lists the mourners and pall-bearers.

173   "Thayer Memorial urged"—New York *Times*, Aug. 31, 1940. If there are no memorials to Thayer, statues of his fictional slugger abound. Most are copies—from a foot high up to 14 feet—of a 1982 original in bronze by Mark Lundeen of Loveland , Colorado.

175   "That are culturally"—*National Recording Recistry Criteria*, Library of Congress, 16.

177   "Mr. Hopper has been"—*Victor Records Sales Catalogue*, 1913, p. 24 (copy at Mills Music Library, Univ. of Wisconsin, Madison), which also lists the 1913 re-issue. The Victor's assigned numbers for the records are: 1906—31559; 1913—35290; 1926—35783. The admission in the 1906 ad copy that Hopper had to be "persuaded" to cut the record reflects his having earlier refused in order to protect the stage value of his famous specialty number.

BIBLIOGRAPHY

NEWSPAPERS: of prime importance in the story of *Casey* are the newspapers of the day, preserving much vital information otherwise forgotten. These are fully identified in the Notes, so receive no mention here.

Anson, A., *A Ballplayer's Career*, Chicago, 1900.

Appel, N., *Slide, Kelly, Slide: The Wild Life and Times of Mike 'King' Kelly, Baseball's First Superstar*, Scarecrow Press, 1996.

Austin, A., "75 Years Ago," *New York Times Magazine*, June 9, 1963.

Berrigan, D., "The Truth About Casey," *Saturday Evening Post*, July 3, 1945.

Bordman, G., *American Musical Theater*, Oxford, 2001.

Burke, J., *Duet In Diamonds: Lillian Russell and Diamond Jim Brady*, Putnam, 1972.

Caren, E., *Baseball Extra: A Newspaper History of Baseball*, Castle Books, 2000.

Cox, J., "When Fans Roared 'Slide, Kelly, Slide' at the Old Ball Game", *Smithsonian*, Oct. 1982.

Croy, H., "Casey At the Bat," *Baseball Magazine*, October, 1908.

Frick, J., *New York's First Theatrical Center: The Rialto at Union Square*, Univ. of Michigan Press, 1985.

Frohman, D., *Daniel Frohman Presents*, 1935.

Ganzl, K., *Encyclopedia of the Musical Theater*, Scenium Books, 2001.

Gardner, M., *The Annotated Casey at the Bat: A Collection of Ballads About the Mighty Casey*, University of Chicago Press, 1984.

Glenister, J., "Who Wrote 'Casey at the Bat'?" *Baseball Magazine*, June 1908

Golden, J., *Stage Struck*, 1930.

Goldstein, W., *Playing for Keeps: A History of Early Baseball*, Cornell University Press, 1989.

Goodwin, N., *Nat Goodwin's Book*, Badger, Boston, 1914.

Hopper, DeWolf, *Once a Clown Always A Clown*, Garden City Co., 1925.

Johnson, B., "Slide, Kelly, Slide"—Baseball As I Knew It," *Saturday Evening Post*, April 12, 1930.

Kelly, M., *Play Ball: Stories of the Diamond Field*, Boston, 1888.

Koppett, L., "The Day 'Casey' First Appeared," *Baseball Digest*, February, 1962.

Leslie, A., *Some Players* [actors], Stone, Chicago, 1901.

Mahony, P., "Ernest Thayer at the Bat," *Noticias*, Winter, 1978.

McCabe. J., *New York City By Sunlight and Gaslight*, Philadelphia, 1882.

Moore, J., and Vermilyea, N. , *Ernest Thayer's 'Casey at the Bat', Background and Characters of Baseball's Most Famous Poem*, McFarland, 1994.

Morell, P., *Lillian Russell: the Era of Plush*, Random House, 1940.

Morris, L., *Incredible New York, 1850–1950*. Random House, 1951.

Mote, J., *Everything Baseball*, Prentice-Hall, 1989.

Murdock, E., *Mighty Casey: All-American*, Greenwood Press, 1984.

Norton, R., *A Chronology of American Musical Theater*, Oxford, 2002.

Odell, G., *Annals of the New York Stage*, Columbia University Press, 1930.

Park, R., "*The Man Who Made Casey Famous*," in *The Hero In Transition*, Ed. Ray Browne, Bowling Green University Press, 1983.

Peck, H., "Who Wrote 'Casey At the Bat'?" *The Scrap Book*, Dec. 1908.

Phelps, W., *What I Like in Poetry*, Scribner's, 1934.

Pearson, D., *Baseball in 1889*, Bowling Green University Press, 1993.

Powers, J., *Twinkle Little Star*, Milwaukee, 1939.

Russell, L., "Reminiscences," *Cosmopolitan*, April-September, 1922.

Santayana, G., *Persons and Places*, MIT Press, 1944.

Seymour, H., *Baseball, the Early Years*, Oxford, 1960.

Smith, H., *First Nights and First Editions*, Little, Brown, 1931.

Smith, R., *Baseball*, Simon & Schuster, 1947.

Spalding, A., *America's National Game*, New York, 1911.

Thorn, J., and Palmer, P., *Total Baseball*, Warner, 1999.

Tieman, R., et. al., *Baseball's First Stars*, Society For Baseball Research, Cleveland, 1996.

Tyler, G., *Whatever Goes Up*, Bobbs, 1934.

Voigt, D., *American Baseball: From Gentleman's Sport to the Commissioner System*, University of Oklahoma Press, 1966.

Wallack, L., *Memories of Fifty Years in the Theater*, New York, 1889.

Ward, J., "Notes of A Baseballist," *Lippincott's*, August, 1886.

Ward, J., *Baseball: How to Become a Player, with the Origin and History of the Game*, Philadelphia, 1888.

Wiles, T., "The Case for Casey," All-Star Game Official Program, 1996, pp. 74-82; Major League Baseball, Inc., New York City.

Wilson, F., *Francis Wilson's Life of Himself*, Houghton, 1924.

ACKNOWLEDGMENTS

M Y FIRST DEBT, A GREAT ONE, IN RESEARCHING THIS STORY is owed to a phalanx of writers long since gone: the newsmen who reported on the professional baseball and Broadway theatrical scenes and doings of the 1880s. To them, and to the periodical and book writers remembering those times, I and grateful: see the bibliography.

More specifically for various kinds of aid and sympathy in research I thank:

At the Mills Music Library, Univ. of Wisconsin—Madison, Director Geri Laudati, and Ass't Dir. Steve Sundell.

At Memorial Library, Univ. of Wisconsin—Madison, the cheerfully efficient staff, with a special nod to its unrivalled resources.

At the Baseball Hall of Fame in Cooperstown, N.Y., Tim Wiles and Claudette Burke.

At the Univ. of Wisconsin Film Archive, Madison, archivist Dorinda Hartman.

At the Monroe (Wisc.) Public Library, Barbara Brewer, Dir., librarians Ann Mueller, Linda Bourquin, Maggie

Guralski, Nancy Myers, Donna Oxenreider, and Rita Grinnell.

At the Worcester, Mass., *Telegram-Gazette*, Greg Labonte.

At The Overlook Press, my able editor David Shoemaker.

INDEX

Page numbers in *italic* refer to illustration in text.